THE
ENTREPRENEWYEAR
PLAN

This belongs to:

_____

If lost, please call or email:

_____

JULLIEN
GORDON
Speaker | Business Coach | Author

THE
FREEDOM
SCHOOL

FORTUNE 500 COMPANIES PLAN & REPORT QUARTERLY

How do you plan on making a fortune without a business plan and goals more specific than "make more money?"

Allow me to help you create a bulletproof business plan that will guide you toward your big goals over the next 365 days.

WWW.THEFREEDOMSCHOOL.COM

INTRODUCTION

The entrepreneurial rat race ends today!

The leap from employee to become an entrepreneur is a courageous one and I celebrate you. You likely left your job because you outgrew your cubicle, literally and figuratively, and you desired more time and financial freedom. At the same time, you also knew you had to hustle to make this new idea work. While most people starting a business call themselves entrepreneurs, there is a step between employee and entrepreneur that many people get stuck on: self-employed. Most solopreneurs aren't true entrepreneurs yet—they are self-employed. Instead of having a job that someone else created for them, they have created a job for themselves.

Being self-employed is difficult. Everything is up to you. While you have autonomy, you no longer have accountability. While you have passion, you no longer have people to help you execute. The absence of a consistent predictable paycheck can quickly lead to a fear-based mindset of scarcity. And at that point, most self-employed people become scavengers and your business becomes a constant hunt for money instead of your passion.

When I first started, I fell into that trap too. I quickly found myself in the entrepreneurial rat race chasing the cheese. I was so busy running after clients and checks that I never stopped to evaluate, strategize, and plan. I was always working in my business, therefore, I didn't have the time to work on my business.

The EntrepreNewYear Plan is designed to free you from that pattern so that your business can have a breakthrough by offering you a simple structured way to plan out the next 365 days of work in 5 hours. As CEO of your company, you can't think like an employee with a 100% ownership stake. You are the driver of your company, not the engine. Therefore you must see the vision, plan for it, and steer everything toward its fulfillment.

MY BUSINESS

PROFIT PIPELINE

Directions: Declare your offerings, quantity sold, and price to get your annual profits.

Profit Pipeline

ENGAGEMENT	NUMBER	PRICE	REVENUE
Facebook Fan + Twitter Followers	3,000 —	$0	$0
Lead Magnet (e.g. PDF, webinar, etc)	1,000	$0	$0
Self-Published Book	100	$10	$1,000
Live or Online Events	100	$100	$10,000
Speaking Engagements	10	$3,000	$30,000
Premium Online Course	20	$1,000	$20,000
Mastermind Group	20	$1,200	$24,000
Coaching Program	5	$3,000	$15,000
			$100,000

B.P.A.I.D. PROGRAM

© Jullien Gordon

The Average Business Cycle (ABC)

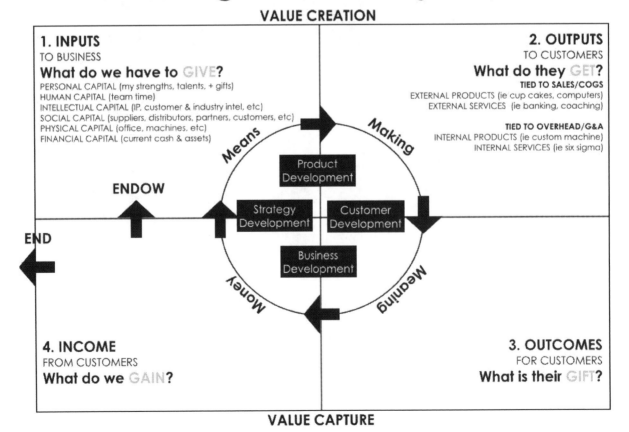

VALUE CREATION

1. INPUTS
TO BUSINESS
What do we have to GIVE?
PERSONAL CAPITAL (my strengths, talents, + gifts)
HUMAN CAPITAL (team time)
INTELLECTUAL CAPITAL (IP, customer & industry intel, etc)
SOCIAL CAPITAL (suppliers, distributors, partners, customers, etc)
PHYSICAL CAPITAL (office, machines. etc)
FINANCIAL CAPITAL (current cash & assets)

2. OUTPUTS
TO CUSTOMERS
What do they GET?
TIED TO SALES/COGS
EXTERNAL PRODUCTS (ie cup cakes, computers)
EXTERNAL SERVICES (ie banking, coaching)

TIED TO OVERHEAD/G&A
INTERNAL PRODUCTS (ie custom machine)
INTERNAL SERVICES (ie six sigma)

ENDOW

Means

Making

Product Development

Strategy Development

Customer Development

Business Development

END

Money

Meaning

4. INCOME
FROM CUSTOMERS
What do we GAIN?

3. OUTCOMES
FOR CUSTOMERS
What is their GIFT?

VALUE CAPTURE

Directions: Fill in the following fields based on the Average Business Cycle and Profit Pipeline.

INPUTS: Everything you will use to create, market, sale, and delivery your products and services

Personal Capital	
Intellectual Capital	
Social Capital	
Physical Capital	
Human Capital	
Financial Capital	

OUTCOMES: The transformation in your customers' businesses or lives as a results of working with you

Target Market	
Results We Create For Our Clients	1. 2. 3.
3 Things That Make Us Unique	1. 2. 3.

OUTPUTS: Your products and services

Product/Service	Quantity ↓	x	Price ↑		Cost		Annual Profit
1		x	$0 / FREE	-	$	=	$
2		x	$	-	$	=	$
3		x	$	-	$	=	$
4		x	$	-	$	=	$
5		x	$	-	$	=	$
6		x	$	-	$	=	$
7		x	$	-	$	=	$
8		x	$	-	$	=	$
9		x	$	-	$	=	$
10		x	$	-	$	=	$
INCOME: The reward you receive for the transformation you created						=	$

WEEKLY DASHBOARD

Directions: Choose your top 6 success metrics that you want to track weekly. Add them to the top of each column in order of importance. Each week, fill in your dashboard so that you can see your progress throughout the year.

Wk.	Date	Metric 1 New Sales	Metric 2 New Leads	Metric 3	Metric 4	Metric 5
1						
2						
3						
4						
5						
6						
7						
8						
9						
10						
11						
12						
13						
14						
15						
16						
17						
18						
19						
20						
21						
22						
23						
24						
25						

Wk.	Date	Metric 1 New Sales	Metric 2 New Leads	Metric 3	Metric 4	Metric 5
26						
27						
28						
29						
30						
31						
32						
33						
34						
35						
36						
37						
38						
39						
40						
41						
42						
43						
44						
45						
46						
47						
48						
49						
50						
51						
52						

MY PROGRESS REPORT

Directions: Using the insights, ideas, and images that came up during your Success Article, identify the 5 to 10 most important metrics in your business and document where they were a year ago, where they are today, and where you want them to be a year from now. This is an opportunity to celebrate this year's success.

Metrics: Measurable Success Metric or Area of Change	Point A: Where I Was Last Year (e.g. Dec 31, 2016)
Book sales	*1st draft complete*
Customers (e.g. satisfaction, repeat, frequency, net promoter score)	
Marketing (e.g # of channels, cost er lead, partnerships)	
Sales (e.g. conversion rate, customer acquisition costs)	
Products & Services (e.g. suite, SKUs, COGS, delivery time)	
Systems & Technology (e.g. automation, adoption, custom coding)	
People & Team (e.g. size, new hires, contractors, suppliers/vendors)	
Financial (e.g. revenues, profits, COGS, run rate)	
My Leadership (e.g. change in style, delegation and empowerment)	
Other:	
Other:	
Other:	
Other:	

Today

A Year From Today

Point B:
Where I Am Today (e.g. Dec 31, 2017)

Point C:
Where I Want To Be Next Year (e.g. Dec 31, 2018)

Published and 2K pre-sold during launch

10,000 more sold + 12 keynote speeches

SUCCESS ARTICLE

Directions: Imagine that *Forbes, Entrepreneur,* or *Inc. Magazine* decided to feature you on the cover after you had an amazing year (this upcoming year). Pretend that it is 365 days from today in the future and write an article from the perspective of the journalist describing the amazing accomplishments of your business during this upcoming year with four success stories—including two actual success stories from this past year and two from your future dream clients this upcoming year.

_____

_____

_____

_____

_____

_____

_____

_____

_____

_____

_____

_____

_____

_____

_____

_____

_____

_____

_____

_____

Last Year Actual Success Story #1

" _____
_____
_____
_____ "

1st Name: _____ Client Type: _____

Last Year Actual Success Story #2

" _____
_____
_____
_____ "

1st Name: _____ Client Type: _____

This Upcoming Year Aspirational Success Story #1

" _____
_____
_____
_____ "

1st Name: _____ Client Type: _____

This Upcoming Year Aspirational Success Story #2

" _____
_____
_____
_____ "

1st Name: _____ Client Type: _____

OFFER TO INCOME

Directions: Turn back to page 2 and pick a product or service you want to grow and use the worksheet below to determine what you need to do to update or create, market, sell, and deliver the product or service you plan to expand this year.

In order to sell _____ _____
                    Quantity   **Product/Service**

at an average price of $_____ for a total annual revenue of $_____
                            Price   **Quantity x Price**

I need a marketing plan and sales strategy that will reach at least _____ people.
                                                                    # of People Who See Offer

My to do list to **update or create** the product/service includes:

❏ _____

❏ _____

❏ _____

❏ _____

My to do list to **market** the product/service includes:

❏ _____

❏ _____

❏ _____

❏ _____

My to do list to **sell** the product/service includes:

❏ _____

❏ _____

❏ _____

❏ _____

My to do list to **deliver** the product/service includes:

❏ _____

❏ _____

❏ _____

❏ _____

Directions: Turn back to page 2 and pick a product or service you want to grow and use the worksheet below to determine what you need to do to update or create, market, sell, and deliver the product or service you plan to expand this year.

In order to sell _____ _____
Quantity   **Product/Service**

at an average price of $_____ for a total annual revenue of $_____
         Price   **Quantity x Price**

I need a marketing plan and sales strategy that will reach at least _____ people.
           # of People Who See Offer

My to do list to **update or create** the product/service includes:

☐ _____

☐ _____

☐ _____

☐ _____

My to do list to **market** the product/service includes:

☐ _____

☐ _____

☐ _____

☐ _____

My to do list to **sell** the product/service includes:

☐ _____

☐ _____

☐ _____

☐ _____

My to do list to **deliver** the product/service includes:

☐ _____

☐ _____

☐ _____

☐ _____

DESIRED EXPERIENCES

Directions: List all of the front stage experiences you want to have this year in your business. Be as specific as possible and focus more on who you have to be become to get where you want to go and have what you want.

Customers How you want your relationship to your customers to be and look:

I/we ultimately want to experience what it is like to be/have...

Examples: loyal rabid repeat customers; a company that customers engage with every day

---

Marketing How you want your marketing to occur to you and others:

I/we ultimately want to experience what it is like to be/have...

Examples: an automated marketing system; new leads coming in through social media

---

Sales How you want your sales to occur to you and others:

I/we ultimately want to experience what it is like to be/have...

Examples: overbooked/oversold; our marketing be valuable in and of itself

---

Products & Services How you want your offerings to grow:

I/we ultimately want to experience what it is like to be/have...

Examples: pre-sold thousands of products before even producing it; the gold standard

---

Directions: List all of the backstage experiences you want to have in this year in your business. Be as specific as possible and focus more on who you have to be become to get where you want to go and have what you want.

Systems & Technology How you want your company to operate:

I/we ultimately want to experience what it is like to be/have...

Examples: processes for every repeat part of our business; efficient workflows

_____

_____

_____

People & Team How do you want to collaborate and work together?

I/we ultimately want to experience what it is like to be/have...

Examples: a flat open-door organization; win-win relationships with contractors/suppliers

_____

_____

_____

Financial How do you want money to flow in and out of the company?

I/we ultimately want to experience what it is like to be/have...

Examples: profitable; a multi-million dollar company; making money daily

_____

_____

_____

My Leadership How do you want to grow professionally as a leader?

I/we ultimately want to experience what it is like to be/have...

Examples: able to have difficult conversations & delegate; a mentor-manager

_____

_____

_____

MONTHLY RHYTHM

Directions: List all of the frontend activities that you need to do daily, weekly, and/or monthly to create the average 30 day rhythm for the maintenance and momentum of your business.

	Frontend	Monday	Tuesday	Wednesday
W E E K 1	Customers			
	Marketing			
	Sales			
	Prdts & Srvcs			
W E E K 2	Customers			
	Marketing			
	Sales			
	Prdts & Srvcs			
W E E K 3	Customers			
	Marketing			
	Sales			
	Prdts & Srvcs			
W E E K 4	Customers			
	Marketing			
	Sales			
	Prdts & Srvcs			
W E E K 5	Customers			
	Marketing			
	Sales			
	Prdts & Srvcs			

	Thursday	Friday	Saturday	Sunday
WEEK 1				
WEEK 2				
WEEK 3				
WEEK 4				
WEEK 5				

MONTHLY RHYTHM

Directions: List all of the backend activities that you need to do daily, weekly, and/or monthly to create the average 30 day rhythm for the maintenance and momentum of your business.

	Backend	Monday	Tuesday	Wednesday
WEEK 1	Systems & Tech			
	People & Team			
	Financial			
	My Leadership			
WEEK 2	Systems & Tech			
	People & Team			
	Financial			
	My Leadership			
WEEK 3	Systems & Tech			
	People & Team			
	Financial			
	My Leadership			
WEEK 4	Systems & Tech			
	People & Team			
	Financial			
	My Leadership			
WEEK 5	Systems & Tech			
	People & Team			
	Financial			
	My Leadership			

	Thursday	Friday	Saturday	Sunday
WEEK 1				
WEEK 2				
WEEK 3				
WEEK 4				
WEEK 5				

Directions: In the first column of the gantt chart below, there are 16 spaces for your annual goals. For each of the 8 statements on pages 9 and 10, write down 2 goals that will help you have that experience this year. Next, number the goals in chronological order to the best of your ability. Shade in the weeks that you will work toward their completion so that you can see an aerial view of your entire year and how it will unfold.

#	Goals, Projects, Launches, Events, Etc	"Do" Date	____ Quarter January 1	2	3	4	5	February 1	2	3	4	March 1	2	3	4
3	Ex. Launch the new website & app	4/1	▓	▓	▓	▓	▓	▓	▓	▓	▓	▓	▓	▓	▓

____ Quarter			____ Quarter			____ Quarter		
April	May	June	July	August	September	October	November	December
1 2 3 4	1 2 3 4 5	1 2 3 4	1 2 3 4 5	1 2 3 4	1 2 3 4	1 2 3 4 5	1 2 3 4	1 2 3 4

MY BUSINESS ACTIVITIES

Directions: List all of the activities you do for your business in the first column. Next fill in the middle 3 columns. And ultimately, determine whether you should automate, delegate, or keep doing each activity in the upcoming year. If it is a GLM, you should probably keep it. If it is a WHL, you should probably try to delegate it or automate it.

All Of My Business Activities	G - Great / A - Average / W - Weak	L - Love It / I - Indifferent / H - Hate It	M - More / S - Same / L - Less	A - Automate / D - Delegate / K - Keep
product/service development				
sales				
accounting/bookkeeping				
content creation				
strategic planning				
managing people				

Directions: Using the 5 Ways To Worthy Worth, identify where there are opportunities for your business to grow. Your answer will help you find holes and inefficiencies to improve your business and help your clients.

1. Worry Where do you see worry? What is keeping you, your team, or clients up at night?

_____

_____

_____

2. Won't What is the one thing that you, your team, or competitors won't do but could have a huge impact?

_____

_____

_____

3. Waste Where do you see wasted time, talent, money, or other resources by you and your team or your clients?

_____

_____

_____

4. Waiting Where do you see unnecessary waiting in your company, among your team, or by clients?

_____

_____

_____

5. Wishing Where do you hear wishing in yourself, from your team, or from clients?

_____

_____

_____

6. Workaholism Where do you see overwork or overwhelm?

_____

_____

_____

Directions: Document the steps of the journey you see a non-customer taking to become a paying customer. Once you do that, articulate, how you are going to incentivize and encourage them to take each step on that journey so that they begin to trust you and ultimately buy from you so that you can help them achieve their goals.

Their Painful Point A in Life or Business: _____

_____

Their Pleasurable Point B in Life or Business: _____

_____

Steps Of The Customer Journey	How will you drive them to take this action?
Ex. 1. Visit my website	weekly YouTube video, guest posts, webinars with thought leaders
Ex. 2. Subscribe to get my free tool	video intro, popup, sidebar ad on blog, Facebook ads
1. What is the 1st thing you want them to do?	How will you get them to take this action?
2. Then what do you want them to do?	How will you get them to take this action?
3. Then what do you want them to do?	How will you get them to take this action?
4. Then what do you want them to do?	How will you get them to take this action?
5. Then what do you want them to do?	How will you get them to take this action?
6. Then what do you want them to do?	How will you get them to take this action?
7. Then what do you want them to do?	How will you get them to take this action?
8. Then what do you want them to do?	How will you get them to take this action?
9. Then what do you want them to do?	How will you get them to take this action?
10. Then what do you want them to do?	How will you get them to take this action?

❒ Prepare files for accountant to do annual taxes & send 1099s

❒ _____

❒ _____

❒ _____

❒ _____

❒ _____

❒ _____

❒ _____

❒ _____

❒ _____

❒ _____

❒ _____

❒ _____

❒ _____

❒ _____

❒ _____

❒ _____

❒ _____

❒ _____

❒ _____

❒ _____

❒ _____

❒ _____

❒ _____

❒ _____

POINT A: WHERE I AM

1A. EXPERIENCE: I ultimately want to experience what it is like to be...
e.g. debt-free, an entrepreneur, passionate about my work, a daily exerciser

a leader of leaders and created a global movement that empowers millions of people

2A. WHY & WHY NOW: Why is having this experience so important to me beyond just doing it? Why now? Why can't I procrastinate on this?

I have wisdom that I know has transformed people's lives already and I need to reach more people with my message

3A. STARTING POINT: What metrics (*e.g. lbs., $US*), images (*e.g. before-and-after picture*), or words (*e.g. unhappily employed*) describe my starting point?

5 mastermind groups and 150 active players as of now

4A. LIMITING BELIEFS: What limiting beliefs will this experience make me face?
e.g. "I don't have enough...", "I'm not smart enough...", "I need more..."

- People are too busy to meet in person
- I don't know where to find enough leaders

5A. EXCUSES & GAPS: What excuses, escape routes, or gaps do I see/foresee stopping me from creating this experience? *e.g. I was too busy with work*

It wasn't growing fast enough. I was inconsistent. I didn't know how to attract new people.

6A. MY ACTIONS: What are the actions that I am 100% accountable for to create this experience?

☐ *be an ambassador for masterminds by speaking & writing*
☐ *training hundreds of group leaders*
☐
☐

7A. FIRST DOMINO: What is the "first domino?" What's the easiest action I can do in faith right now that will set my experience in motion? *e.g. Send invitations. Pay a coach. Buy my ticket. Give a friend $ if I don't do it.*

☐ **I will** *announce the launch of Masterminds.org in conjunction with the New Year Guide*

POINT B: WHERE I'M GOING

1B. SPECIFIC GOAL: Given the experience I want to have, my goal is to.... *e.g. Eliminate $3,597 in credit card debt. Earn $1,000/month on the side coaching or consulting. Change industry & function. Run a marathon in 4 hours.*

develop 500 mastermind group leaders with over 5,000 members

2B. JOURNEY: How do I want to feel in pursuit of this goal? *e.g joy, challenge, excitement, stretched, loved, abundant, encouraged, mastery, powerful, clarity*

transformed, inspired, motivated, stretched, mastery, aligned purpose, influential, collaborative, trusting, and momentum

3B. EVIDENCE OF SUCCESS: How will I measure & show my success while having this experience? *e.g. lbs. lost, before & after pic, $s earned, # of clients*

# of trained group leaders, # of active players, # of goals set and completed each month

4B. WINNING BELIEFS: What beliefs or affirmations will counter my limiting beliefs? Write the opposite of your limiting belief on the previous page.

+ Nothing is more important to people than living their dream
+ Leaders are everywhere and are looking for a chance to lead

5B. SOLUTIONS & SYSTEMS: How can I address these excuses, escape routes, and gaps in advance? *e.g. Get a coach. Ask for help. Join a group. Take a class.*

☐ Hire someone to manage digital marketing so I can focus
☐ Partner with existing leaders rather than train new ones
☐

6B. MY ACCOUNTABILITY: Who can help me successfully create this experience by serving as a coach, cheerleader, or kick in the butt?

Name(s): A team of 2 dedicated listeners (Amparo & Kazi)

☐ **I made a verbal commitment to them that I would:** commit to finding 2 100 new leaders a day to join our movement as coaches

7B. SIGNATURE: Am I fully committed to making this experience happen now?

Sign Here: Jullien Gordon   **Date:** 1/1/2018

POINT A: WHERE I AM

1A. EXPERIENCE: I ultimately want to experience what it is like to be...
e.g. debt-free, an entrepreneur, passionate about my work, a daily exerciser

_____
_____

2A. WHY & WHY NOW: Why is having this experience so important to me beyond just doing it? Why now? Why can't I procrastinate on this?

_____
_____

3A. STARTING POINT: What metrics (*e.g. lbs., $US*), images (*e.g. before-and-after picture*), or words (*e.g. unhappily employed*) describe my starting point?

_____
_____

4A. LIMITING BELIEFS: What limiting beliefs will this experience make me face?
e.g. "I don't have enough...", "I'm not smart enough...", "I need more..."

- _____
- _____

5A. EXCUSES & GAPS: What excuses, escape routes, or gaps do I see/foresee stopping me from creating this experience? *e.g. I was too busy with work*

_____
_____

6A. MY ACTIONS: What are the actions that I am 100% accountable for to create this experience?

- [ ] _____
- [ ] _____
- [ ] _____
- [ ] _____

7A. FIRST DOMINO: What is the "first domino?" What's the easiest action I can do in faith right now that will set my experience in motion? *e.g. Send invitations. Pay a coach. Buy my ticket. Give a friend $ if I don't do it.*

- [ ] I will _____

POINT B: WHERE I'M GOING

1B. SPECIFIC GOAL: Given the experience I want to have, my goal is to.... *e.g. Eliminate $3,597 in credit card debt. Earn $1,000/month on the side coaching or consulting. Change industry & function. Run a marathon in 4 hours.*

_____

_____

2B. JOURNEY: How do I want to feel in pursuit of this goal? *e.g joy, challenge, excitement, stretched, loved, abundant, encouraged, mastery, powerful, clarity*

_____

_____

3B. EVIDENCE OF SUCCESS: How will I measure & show my success while having this experience? *e.g. lbs. lost, before & after pic, $s earned, # of clients*

_____

_____

4B. WINNING BELIEFS: What beliefs or affirmations will counter my limiting beliefs? Write the opposite of your limiting belief on the previous page.

+ _____

+ _____

5B. SOLUTIONS & SYSTEMS: How can I address these excuses, escape routes, and gaps in advance? e.g. *Get a coach. Ask for help. Join a group. Take a class.*

☐ _____

☐ _____

☐ _____

6B. MY ACCOUNTABILITY: Who can help me successfully create this experience by serving as a coach, cheerleader, or kick in the butt?

Name(s): _____

☐ I made a verbal commitment to them that I would:_____

_____

7B. SIGNATURE: Am I fully committed to making this experience happen now?

Sign Here: _____ Date: _____

POINT A: WHERE I AM

1A. EXPERIENCE: I ultimately want to experience what it is like to be...
e.g. debt-free, an entrepreneur, passionate about my work, a daily exerciser

_____

_____

2A WHY & WHY NOW: Why is having this experience so important to me beyond just doing it? Why now? Why can't I procrastinate on this?

_____

_____

3A. STARTING POINT: What metrics (*e.g. lbs., $US*), images (*e.g. before-and-after picture*), or words (*e.g. unhappily employed*) describe my starting point?

_____

_____

4A. LIMITING BELIEFS: What limiting beliefs will this experience make me face?
e.g. "I don't have enough...", "I'm not smart enough...", "I need more..."

- _____

- _____

5A. EXCUSES & GAPS: What excuses, escape routes, or gaps do I see/foresee stopping me from creating this experience? *e.g. I was too busy with work*

_____

_____

6A. MY ACTIONS: What are the actions that I am 100% accountable for to create this experience?

☐ _____

☐ _____

☐ _____

☐ _____

7A. FIRST DOMINO: What is the "first domino?" What's the easiest action I can do in faith right now that will set my experience in motion? *e.g. Send invitations. Pay a coach. Buy my ticket. Give a friend $ if I don't do it.*

☐ I will _____

_____

POINT B: WHERE I'M GOING

1B. SPECIFIC GOAL: Given the experience I want to have, my goal is to.... *e.g. Eliminate $3,597 in credit card debt. Earn $1,000/month on the side coaching or consulting. Change industry & function. Run a marathon in 4 hours.*

_____

_____

2B. JOURNEY: How do I want to feel in pursuit of this goal? *e.g joy, challenge, excitement, stretched, loved, abundant, encouraged, mastery, powerful, clarity*

_____

_____

3B. EVIDENCE OF SUCCESS: How will I measure & show my success while having this experience? *e.g. lbs. lost, before & after pic, $s earned, # of clients*

_____

_____

4B. WINNING BELIEFS: What beliefs or affirmations will counter my limiting beliefs? Write the opposite of your limiting belief on the previous page.

+ _____

+ _____

5B. SOLUTIONS & SYSTEMS: How can I address these excuses, escape routes, and gaps in advance? e.g. *Get a coach. Ask for help. Join a group. Take a class.*

☐ _____

☐ _____

☐ _____

6B. MY ACCOUNTABILITY: Who can help me successfully create this experience by serving as a coach, cheerleader, or kick in the butt?

Name(s): _____

☐ **I made a verbal commitment to them that I would:** _____

_____

7B. SIGNATURE: Am I fully committed to making this experience happen now?

Sign Here: _____ Date: _____

"THE BEST WAY TO PREDICT THE FUTURE IS TO CREATE IT."

MY PLANNER

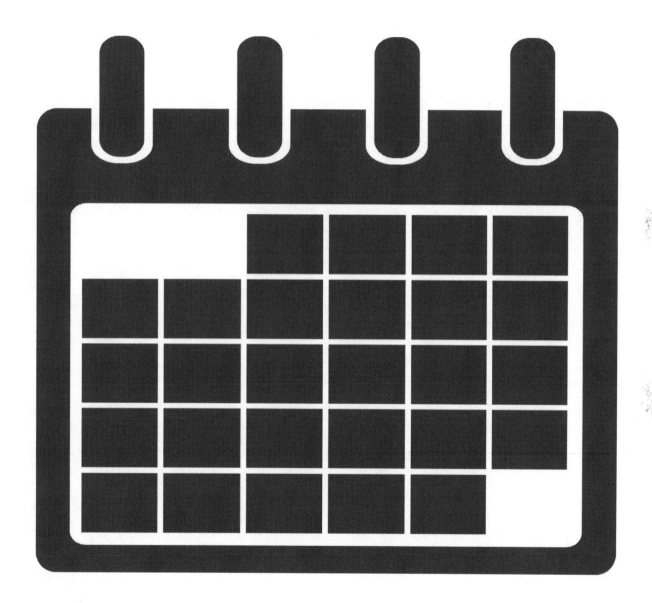

WEEKLY PLANNING

My purpose is to help you experience more freedom in your business and life. And this tool was created with that purpose in mind.

I am a recovering workaholic. I could manage my time and be busy, but I couldn't manage my life. My work spilled into and intoxicated my personal life, damaging relationships that I said were important to me and my health.

The EntrepreNewYear Plan is a weekly process and set of tools that I have been using to shift from workaholic to high performer in my personal and professional life. It's not just about time management. It's about time leadership and energy management.

The difference between high performers and workaholics can appear subtle. They both work hard. But high performers work hard in healthy, sustainable ways that leave them fulfilled and happy. A workaholic works hard in unhealthy, unsustainable ways that leave them empty and unhappy.

This system is about lifestyle design. Time management is a natural derivative of lifestyle design since we experience life between time and space. This system has helped me become more intentional about the design my life by using weeks, days, and hours as the unit of change. And because of this system, I believe that when you change your day, you ultimately change your life.

Time is the most valuable asset we have. It's even more precious than money. Money comes and goes. Time just goes and never comes back. And no amount of money can earn you another second of time. Ironically, we track our money through bank accounts and budgets, but we don't track our time. And every week, we each get 168 hours of time to invest, but many people end up wasting time or killing time thus earning no return on life.

So every Sunday evening, I pay myself first by setting intentions for how I'm going to invest my time in people, projects, and problems that are important to me. I spend 15 minutes creating a vision for my upcoming week and then at the beginning of each work day I evaluate and edit my visions and intentions as life occurs.

This isn't to be rigid or to fill the 168 hours ahead with busy activity. In fact, it's quite the opposite. This process allows me to know:

- When and where I can be flexible after putting my highest priorities first (e.g. family and meaningful work)

- How I spend each hour of my week so I can determine whether those activities are actually leading to business (which is different than being busy)

- When and what I need to say "No" to in order to keep my commitments and live my values

Too often, a week flies by and we can't recall what we did or what we accomplished. The EntrepreNewYear Plan will help you to weekly document and track your progress on your personal and professional goals. Like a mirror, it will reflect back to you with total honesty how effective and efficient you are truly being and from there you can make new choices that move you toward who you know you can become.

When you look back on your life and consider whether it was successful, the easiest way to know will be to examine how you chose to spend your time.

I can't guarantee you more time, but I believe that The EntrepreNewYear Plan will help you ensure that the precious hours you do have are filled with more joy and freedom.

Wishing you more degrees of freedom,

Jullien Gordon

Your Intention

The x-factor to success is knowing your why. The clearer you are on your intention before beginning anything, the more likely it is that you will achieve what you set out to accomplish. There are several ways to use The EntrepreNewYear Plan and I want you to choose what you want from it in advance.

My primary intention for using this tool is to...
❏ Envision my week ❏ Track my time ❏ Manage my to do list ❏ Keep my daily rituals

I am using this tool to become a high performing... ❏ Entrepreneur ❏ Professional ❏ Partner ❏ Parent

I intend to use this tool on... ❏ Weekdays 6a-6p ❏ Weekdays 6p-10p ❏ Weekends

The EntrepreNewYear Plan will... ❏ Stay wherever I go ❏ Stay at my desk ❏ Stay at home

Paper + Technology

There is power in writing that technology can't replace. I encourage you to use pencil in your HPP. While we may set intentions for the next eight hours ahead of us, things happen. Though your schedule may get adjusted, your intentions should remain firm. If you lay out a vision on Monday morning and then at 10am you have to put out a fire, the things you intended to do must be shifted like a Tetris block to a new position in the week ahead.

The EntrepreNewYear Plan is designed to work in conjunction with whatever technology you use for calendaring. The HPP will help you maximize your unintentional time which makes up a majority of our lives. Unintentional time includes the time gaps between the have-tos and hate-tos (meetings, appointments, errands, eating, commuting, etc) that often get wasted because they are unstructured. Your calendar keeps your appointments. Your HPP helps you be intentional about the rest of life in between.

Anchor In Time

When there is a meeting scheduled in our online calendars we tend to show up even if we think it will be a waste of time. Why? Because it is anchored in time. Similarly, all to do list items have a due date or do date and we can anchor them in time to ensure that we show up and they get done.

For instance, let's say that you estimate completing a proposal will take you two hours of quality time. Rather than allowing the words "complete proposal" to linger on a Post-It note, you can simply integrate the two hours needed into your schedule just like a meeting.

Outside of work, we tend to give the people we love most our leftover time and energy. Our jobs get the best of us during the day and then our families get the rest of us. We justify it by telling ourselves that we are working hard for them and that they will always be there.

In the same way that you schedule meetings, you can use The EntrepreNewYear Plan to schedule "meanings" with those you love. Meanings could mean floor time with your infant, date night with your partner, or movie night with the entire family. While people say they don't want to be penciled into your schedule, anchoring those you love in time demonstrates that they are just as important to you as the meeting in your calendar.

First Things First

A high performer is proactive about their time and work. They design their day and anchor the most meaningful and important things in time first, and then they allow fires and other unplanned events to fill in the rest of their day. They don't allow distractions to deter their strategy. The alternative is to be reactive and allow all of the minutia to eat up your time.

The EntpreNewYear Plan has a daily checklist that allows you track how well you are doing at putting first things first. Self-care items that put you and your health first that might go on your daily checklist include gardening, meditate, exercise, read, journal, breakfast, or lunch break. Family items that may go on your daily checklist might include family dinner, toy time or reading with daughter, call or email someone I love, or send a thank you card.

Professional priorities that may go on your daily checklist might include number of sales conversations, affirm a team member, update quarterly KPIs, read an industry-related article, or less than 60 minutes of email. Identify the daily rituals that allow you to perform at your highest level and ensure that you anchor them in time and do them three to seven times per week.

Being Busy vs. Doing Business

Somehow being busy became positively associated with importance and success. As a result, people get uncomfortable when there is literally nothing to do. The goal of The EntrepreNewYear Plan is help you experience more happy hours in your personal and professional life while improving your results. I want to make your life more fulfilling, not fill it with things to do.

High performers tend to work less in terms of time than low performers. They don't buy into the illusion of 110%. They know that 110% is unsustainable. Instead they focus on increasing their capacity so that their 100% is better than the competition's 110%.

Rather than measuring their value by the quantity of time they are working, they measure it by the quality of work they do. Whereas low performers do work to look important, high performers look for important work to do. High performers seek to apply the right effort to the right action at the right time. That's how you create results and maximize value. And that's the difference between doing business and being busy.

Parkinson's Law

Parkinson's Law suggests that work expands to fill space and time. If I give you 60 minutes to do a task that really only takes 30 minutes, you'll likely take 60 minutes to do it. Whereas if I give you the same task, but only 30 minutes, you'll complete it in 30 minutes without compromising the quality or results.

Work expands to fill our day when we don't put boundaries on it. It spills into the next hour and then the next and then other domains of our life after 5pm and on weekends, negatively affecting our personal relationships and ability to live in alignment with our values.

The secret to using Parkinson's Law to your advantage is to shorten the amount of time and space you give yourself to complete tasks. In a sense, it's creating the feeling of procrastination and the pressure that comes with it without having a deadline. This technique allowed me to graduate from college in three years instead of four. By squeezing the space and time, I forced myself to be more productive. The 40-hour workweek is based on an average load, so in off-seasons, don't work more than you really have to just because.

Progress Begets Progress

While Post-it notes are great for reminders and grocery lists they don't serve as effective measurements of progress because they are separate small pieces of paper that are scattered or trashed when we are done with them. The EntrepreNewYear Plan keeps your to do lists and everything you will achieve this year personally and professionally in one place. Over time, you will be able to see your progress rather than feeling like work is just a never-ending to do list. You will never have to stand in the parking lot on a Friday and wonder what you accomplished that day, that week, or that month because it will all be right here.

THE PROCESS

CALENDAR = YOUR VISION
What do I want to achieve? By when?

1.

Use your monthly calendar to document important upcoming events, projects, appointments, and deadlines.

proposals

meetings

trips

JANUARY

Monday	Tuesday	Wednesday	Thursday	Friday	Saturday	Sunday	Notes
			1	2	3	4	
5 9am *Team Mtg*	6 10am *Follow-Ups*	7 6pm *Date Night*	8 11am *Coach Call*	9 *Annual Report Due*	10	11	
12 9am *Team Mtg*	13 *Mike's Birthday* 10am *Follow-Ups*	14 6pm *Date Night*	15 *Jamaica Trip*	16 *Jamaica Trip*	17 *Jamaica Trip* *Gabby's Wedding*	18 *Jamaica Trip*	
19 9am *Team Mtg*	20 *Inc. Proposal Due* 10am *Follow-Ups*	21 6pm *Date Night*	22 11am *Coach Call*	23 *Sales Conference*	24 *Mechanic*	25	
26 9am *Team Mtg* 5pm *Dentist*	27 10am *Follow-Ups*	28 6pm *Date Night*	29 1pm *Board Mtg*	30 *Chris' Birthday* *Pay Bills* 5pm *Doctor*	31		

events

reports

projects

deadlines

NOTE: USE YOUR ONLINE CALENDAR

THE PROCESS

TO DO LIST = YOUR STRATEGY
What do I have to do to achieve it?

2.
Calculate your profit from last week and YTD and define what's working and what isn't.

3.
Add daily and weekly rituals and keep track during the week.

4.
Based on your monthly calendar, identify what your top priorities are this week.

5.
Based on your top priorities, list the next best actions or to do list in order or priority.

6.
Make a list of other things you need to do this week as well as the things you need to follow up on.

7.
Document how you've grown or what you're grateful for in each area of your life.

8.
Plan out your meals for the week and what you intend to do this upcoming weekend.

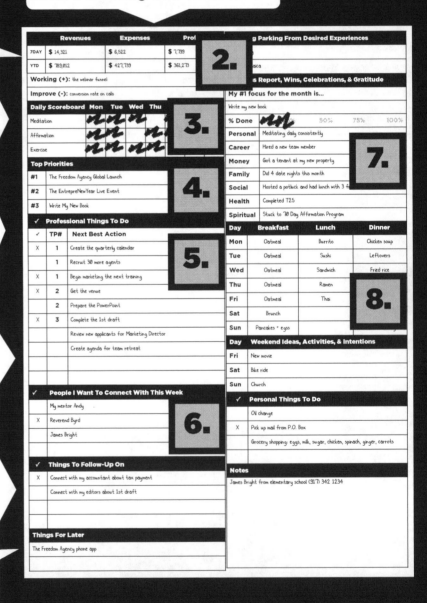

THE PROCESS

WEEKLY TIME GRID = YOUR PLAN
How should I invest my time accordingly?

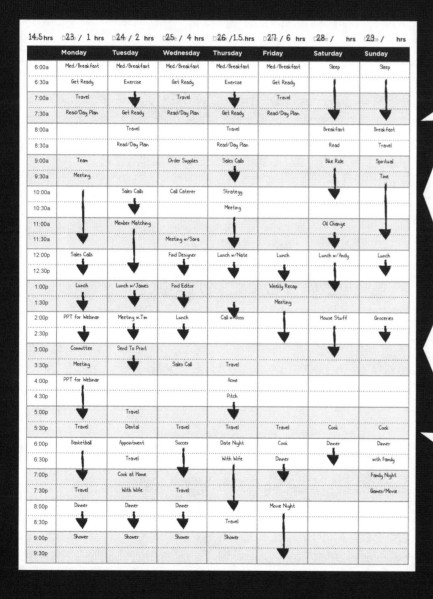

8.

Fill-in or black-out things you do daily such as sleep, eat, travel, exercise, and shower.

9.

Using your calendar, black-out all scheduled events, meetings, appointments, and have-tos.

10.

With the time you have left, fill-in the gaps in your schedule with the items from your to do list starting with your highest priorities first.

11.

After each 30 minute time slot, update your time grid to reflect what you actually did and adjust your plan accordingly.

	Revenues	Expenses	Profits
7DAY	$ 14,321	$ 6,522	$ 7,799
YTD	$ 789,012	$ 427,739	$ 361,273

Working (+): the webinar funnel

Improve (-): conversion rate on calls

Daily Scoreboard	Mon	Tue	Wed	Thu	Fri	Sat	Sun
Meditation	✓	✓	✓	✓	✓		
Affirmation	✓	✓		✓	✓		
Exercise	✓	✓	✓	✓		✓	

Top Priorities

#1	The Freedom Agency Global Launch
#2	The EntrepreNewYear Live Event
#3	Write My New Book

✓ Professional Things To Do

✓	TP#	Next Best Action
X	1	Create the quarterly calendar
	1	Recruit 30 more agents
X	1	Begin marketing the next training
X	2	Get the venue
	2	Prepare the PowerPoint
X	3	Complete the 1st draft
		Review new applicants for Marketing Director
		Create agenda for team retreat

✓ People I Want To Connect With This Week

	My mentor Andy
X	Reverend Byrd
	James Bright

✓ Things To Follow-Up On

X	Connect with my accountant about tax payment
	Connect with my editors about 1st draft

Things For Later

The Freedom Agency phone app

Planning Parking From Desired Experiences

Apple picking

Trip to Jamaica

Progress Report, Wins, Celebrations, & Gratitude

My #1 focus for the month is...

Write my new book

% Done	✓✓ 25%	50%	75%	100%
Personal	Meditating daily consistently			
Career	Hired a new team member			
Money	Got a tenant at my new property			
Family	Did 4 date nights this month			
Social	Hosted a potluck and had lunch with 3 friends			
Health	Completed T25			
Spiritual	Stuck to 70 Day Affirmation Program			

Day	Breakfast	Lunch	Dinner
Mon	Oatmeal	Burrito	Chicken soup
Tue	Oatmeal	Sushi	Leftovers
Wed	Oatmeal	Sandwich	Fried rice
Thu	Oatmeal	Ramen	Date Night
Fri	Oatmeal	Thai	Leftovers
Sat	Brunch		Potluck
Sun	Pancakes + eggs		Pizza w/ family

Day	Weekend Ideas, Activities, & Intentions
Fri	New movie
Sat	Bike ride
Sun	Church

✓ Personal Things To Do

	Oil change
X	Pick up mail from P.O. Box
	Grocery shopping: eggs, milk, sugar, chicken, spinach, ginger, carrots

Notes

James Bright from elementary school (917) 342 1234

14.5 hrs	23 / 1 hrs	24 / 2 hrs	25 / 4 hrs	26 / 1.5 hrs	27 / 6 hrs	28 / hrs	29 / hrs
	Monday	**Tuesday**	**Wednesday**	**Thursday**	**Friday**	**Saturday**	**Sunday**
6:00a	Med./Breakfast	Med./Breakfast	Med./Breakfast	Med./Breakfast	Med./Breakfast	Sleep	Sleep
6:30a	Get Ready	Exercise	Get Ready	Exercise	Get Ready	↓	↓
7:00a	Travel	↓	Travel	↓	Travel		
7:30a	Read/Day Plan	Get Ready	Read/Day Plan	Get Ready	Read/Day Plan	↓	↓
8:00a		Travel		Travel		Breakfast	Breakfast
8:30a		Read/Day Plan		Read/Day Plan		Read	Travel
9:00a	Team		Order Supplies	Sales Calls		Bike Ride	Spiritual
9:30a	Meeting			↓		↓	Time
10:00a	↓	Sales Calls	Call Caterer	Strategy			↓
10:30a		↓		Meeting			
11:00a		Member Matching		↓		Oil Change	↓
11:30a	↓	↓	Meeting w/Sara			↓	
12:00p	Sales Calls		Find Designer	Lunch w/Nate	Lunch	Lunch w/Andy	Lunch
12:30p	↓	↓	↓	↓	↓		↓
1:00p	Lunch	Lunch w/James	Find Editor		Weekly Recap	↓	
1:30p	↓	↓	↓	↓	Meeting		
2:00p	PPT for Webinar	Meeting w.Tim	Lunch	Call w/Boss		House Stuff	Groceries
2:30p	↓	↓	↓		↓		↓
3:00p	Committee	Send To Print				↓	
3:30p	Meeting	↓	Sales Call	Travel			
4:00p	PPT for Webinar			Acme			
4:30p				Pitch			
5:00p	↓	Travel		↓			
5:30p	Travel	Dental	Travel	Travel	Travel	Cook	Cook
6:00p	Basketball	Appointment	Soccer	Date Night	Cook	Dinner	Dinner
6:30p		Travel	↓	With Wife	Dinner	↓	with Family
7:00p	↓	Cook at Home	↓	↓	↓		Family Night
7:30p	Travel	With Wife	Travel				Games/Movie
8:00p	Dinner	Dinner	Dinner	↓	Movie Night		
8:30p	↓	↓	↓	Travel	↓		
9:00p	Shower	Shower	Shower	Shower			
9:30p				↓			

ENTREPRENEWYEAR.COM | THE ENTREPRENEWYEAR PLAN

	Revenues	Expenses	Profits
7DAY	$	$	$
YTD	$	$	$

Working (+):

Improve (-):

Daily Scoreboard	Mon	Tue	Wed	Thu	Fri	Sat	Sun

Top Priorities

#1	
#2	
#3	

✓ Professional Things To Do

✓	TP#	Next Best Action
	1	
	1	
	1	
	2	
	2	
	3	

✓ People I Want To Connect With This Week

✓ Things To Follow-Up On

Things For Later

Planning Parking From Desired Experiences

Progress Report, Wins, Celebrations, & Gratitude

My #1 focus for the month is...

% Done	25%	50%	75%	100%
Personal				
Career				
Money				
Family				
Social				
Health				
Spiritual				

Day	Breakfast	Lunch	Dinner
Mon			
Tue			
Wed			
Thu			
Fri			
Sat			
Sun			

Day	Weekend Ideas, Activities, & Intentions
Fri	
Sat	
Sun	

✓ Personal Things To Do

Notes

Tot **hrs**	Date /	**hrs**	Date /	**hrs**	Date /	**hrs**	Date /	**hrs**	Date /	**hrs**	Date /	**hrs**	Date /	**hrs**
	Monday		**Tuesday**		**Wednesday**		**Thursday**		**Friday**		**Saturday**		**Sunday**	
6:00a														
6:30a														
7:00a														
7:30a														
8:00a														
8:30a														
9:00a														
9:30a														
10:00a														
10:30a														
11:00a														
11:30a														
12:00p														
12:30p														
1:00p														
1:30p														
2:00p														
2:30p														
3:00p														
3:30p														
4:00p														
4:30p														
5:00p														
5:30p														
6:00p														
6:30p														
7:00p														
7:30p														
8:00p														
8:30p														
9:00p														
9:30p														

	Revenues	Expenses	Profits
7DAY	$	$	$
YTD	$	$	$

Working (+):

Improve (-):

Daily Scoreboard	Mon	Tue	Wed	Thu	Fri	Sat	Sun

Top Priorities

#1	
#2	
#3	

✓ Professional Things To Do

✓	TP#	Next Best Action
	1	
	1	
	1	
	2	
	2	
	3	

✓ People I Want To Connect With This Week

✓ Things To Follow-Up On

Things For Later

Planning Parking From Desired Experiences

Progress Report, Wins, Celebrations, & Gratitude

My #1 focus for the month is...

% Done	25%	50%	75%	100%
Personal				
Career				
Money				
Family				
Social				
Health				
Spiritual				

Day	Breakfast	Lunch	Dinner
Mon			
Tue			
Wed			
Thu			
Fri			
Sat			
Sun			

Day	Weekend Ideas, Activities, & Intentions
Fri	
Sat	
Sun	

✓ Personal Things To Do

Notes

Tot hrs	Date / hrs	Date / hrs	Date / hrs	Date / hrs	Date / hrs	Date / hrs	Date / hrs
	Monday	Tuesday	Wednesday	Thursday	Friday	Saturday	Sunday
6:00a							
6:30a							
7:00a							
7:30a							
8:00a							
8:30a							
9:00a							
9:30a							
10:00a							
10:30a							
11:00a							
11:30a							
12:00p							
12:30p							
1:00p							
1:30p							
2:00p							
2:30p							
3:00p							
3:30p							
4:00p							
4:30p							
5:00p							
5:30p							
6:00p							
6:30p							
7:00p							
7:30p							
8:00p							
8:30p							
9:00p							
9:30p							

	Revenues	Expenses	Profits
7DAY	$	$	$
YTD	$	$	$

Working (+):

Improve (-):

Daily Scoreboard	Mon	Tue	Wed	Thu	Fri	Sat	Sun

Top Priorities

#1	
#2	
#3	

✓ Professional Things To Do

✓	TP#	Next Best Action
	1	
	1	
	1	
	2	
	2	
	3	

✓ People I Want To Connect With This Week

✓	

✓ Things To Follow-Up On

✓	

Things For Later

Planning Parking From Desired Experiences

Progress Report, Wins, Celebrations, & Gratitude

My #1 focus for the month is...

% Done	25%	50%	75%	100%
Personal				
Career				
Money				
Family				
Social				
Health				
Spiritual				

Day	Breakfast	Lunch	Dinner
Mon			
Tue			
Wed			
Thu			
Fri			
Sat			
Sun			

Day	Weekend Ideas, Activities, & Intentions
Fri	
Sat	
Sun	

✓ Personal Things To Do

Notes

	Monday	Tuesday	Wednesday	Thursday	Friday	Saturday	Sunday
6:00a							
6:30a							
7:00a							
7:30a							
8:00a							
8:30a							
9:00a							
9:30a							
10:00a							
10:30a							
11:00a							
11:30a							
12:00p							
12:30p							
1:00p							
1:30p							
2:00p							
2:30p							
3:00p							
3:30p							
4:00p							
4:30p							
5:00p							
5:30p							
6:00p							
6:30p							
7:00p							
7:30p							
8:00p							
8:30p							
9:00p							
9:30p							

	Revenues	Expenses	Profits
7DAY	$	$	$
YTD	$	$	$

Working (+):

Improve (-):

Daily Scoreboard	Mon	Tue	Wed	Thu	Fri	Sat	Sun

Top Priorities

#1	
#2	
#3	

✓ Professional Things To Do

✓	TP#	Next Best Action
	1	
	1	
	1	
	2	
	2	
	3	

✓ People I Want To Connect With This Week

✓ Things To Follow-Up On

Things For Later

Planning Parking From Desired Experiences

Progress Report, Wins, Celebrations, & Gratitude

My #1 focus for the month is...

% Done	25%	50%	75%	100%
Personal				
Career				
Money				
Family				
Social				
Health				
Spiritual				

Day	Breakfast	Lunch	Dinner
Mon			
Tue			
Wed			
Thu			
Fri			
Sat			
Sun			

Day	Weekend Ideas, Activities, & Intentions
Fri	
Sat	
Sun	

✓ Personal Things To Do

Notes

Tot **hrs**	Date **/**	**hrs**	Date **/**	**hrs**	Date **/**	**hrs**	Date **/**	**hrs**	Date **/**	**hrs**	Date **/**	**hrs**	Date **/**	**hrs**
	Monday		**Tuesday**		**Wednesday**		**Thursday**		**Friday**		**Saturday**		**Sunday**	
6:00a														
6:30a														
7:00a														
7:30a														
8:00a														
8:30a														
9:00a														
9:30a														
10:00a														
10:30a														
11:00a														
11:30a														
12:00p														
12:30p														
1:00p														
1:30p														
2:00p														
2:30p														
3:00p														
3:30p														
4:00p														
4:30p														
5:00p														
5:30p														
6:00p														
6:30p														
7:00p														
7:30p														
8:00p														
8:30p														
9:00p														
9:30p														

	Revenues	Expenses	Profits
7DAY	$	$	$
YTD	$	$	$

Working (+):

Improve (-):

Daily Scoreboard	Mon	Tue	Wed	Thu	Fri	Sat	Sun

Top Priorities

#1	
#2	
#3	

✓ Professional Things To Do

✓	TP#	Next Best Action
	1	
	1	
	1	
	2	
	2	
	3	

✓ People I Want To Connect With This Week

✓ Things To Follow-Up On

Things For Later

Planning Parking From Desired Experiences

Progress Report, Wins, Celebrations, & Gratitude

My #1 focus for the month is...

% Done	25%	50%	75%	100%
Personal				
Career				
Money				
Family				
Social				
Health				
Spiritual				

Day	Breakfast	Lunch	Dinner
Mon			
Tue			
Wed			
Thu			
Fri			
Sat			
Sun			

Day	Weekend Ideas, Activities, & Intentions
Fri	
Sat	
Sun	

✓ Personal Things To Do

Notes

Tot hrs	Date / hrs	Date / hrs	Date / hrs	Date / hrs	Date / hrs	Date / hrs	Date / hrs
	Monday	**Tuesday**	**Wednesday**	**Thursday**	**Friday**	**Saturday**	**Sunday**
6:00a							
6:30a							
7:00a							
7:30a							
8:00a							
8:30a							
9:00a							
9:30a							
10:00a							
10:30a							
11:00a							
11:30a							
12:00p							
12:30p							
1:00p							
1:30p							
2:00p							
2:30p							
3:00p							
3:30p							
4:00p							
4:30p							
5:00p							
5:30p							
6:00p							
6:30p							
7:00p							
7:30p							
8:00p							
8:30p							
9:00p							
9:30p							

	Revenues	Expenses	Profits
7DAY	$	$	$
YTD	$	$	$

Working (+):
Improve (-):

Daily Scoreboard	Mon	Tue	Wed	Thu	Fri	Sat	Sun

Top Priorities

#1	
#2	
#3	

✓ Professional Things To Do

✓	TP#	Next Best Action
	1	
	1	
	1	
	2	
	2	
	3	

✓ People I Want To Connect With This Week

✓ Things To Follow-Up On

Things For Later

Planning Parking From Desired Experiences

Progress Report, Wins, Celebrations, & Gratitude

My #1 focus for the month is...

% Done	25%	50%	75%	100%
Personal				
Career				
Money				
Family				
Social				
Health				
Spiritual				

Day	Breakfast	Lunch	Dinner
Mon			
Tue			
Wed			
Thu			
Fri			
Sat			
Sun			

Day	Weekend Ideas, Activities, & Intentions
Fri	
Sat	
Sun	

✓ Personal Things To Do

Notes

Tot hrs	Date / hrs	Date / hrs	Date / hrs	Date / hrs	Date / hrs	Date / hrs	Date / hrs
	Monday	**Tuesday**	**Wednesday**	**Thursday**	**Friday**	**Saturday**	**Sunday**
6:00a							
6:30a							
7:00a							
7:30a							
8:00a							
8:30a							
9:00a							
9:30a							
10:00a							
10:30a							
11:00a							
11:30a							
12:00p							
12:30p							
1:00p							
1:30p							
2:00p							
2:30p							
3:00p							
3:30p							
4:00p							
4:30p							
5:00p							
5:30p							
6:00p							
6:30p							
7:00p							
7:30p							
8:00p							
8:30p							
9:00p							
9:30p							

	Revenues	Expenses	Profits
7DAY	$	$	$
YTD	$	$	$

Working (+):

Improve (-):

Daily Scoreboard	Mon	Tue	Wed	Thu	Fri	Sat	Sun

Top Priorities

#1	
#2	
#3	

✓ Professional Things To Do

✓	TP#	Next Best Action
	1	
	1	
	1	
	2	
	2	
	3	

✓ People I Want To Connect With This Week

✓ Things To Follow-Up On

Things For Later

Planning Parking From Desired Experiences

Progress Report, Wins, Celebrations, & Gratitude

My #1 focus for the month is...

% Done	25%	50%	75%	100%
Personal				
Career				
Money				
Family				
Social				
Health				
Spiritual				

Day	Breakfast	Lunch	Dinner
Mon			
Tue			
Wed			
Thu			
Fri			
Sat			
Sun			

Day	Weekend Ideas, Activities, & Intentions
Fri	
Sat	
Sun	

✓ Personal Things To Do

Notes

Tot hrs	Date / hrs	Date / hrs	Date / hrs	Date / hrs	Date / hrs	Date / hrs	Date / hrs
	Monday	Tuesday	Wednesday	Thursday	Friday	Saturday	Sunday
6:00a							
6:30a							
7:00a							
7:30a							
8:00a							
8:30a							
9:00a							
9:30a							
10:00a							
10:30a							
11:00a							
11:30a							
12:00p							
12:30p							
1:00p							
1:30p							
2:00p							
2:30p							
3:00p							
3:30p							
4:00p							
4:30p							
5:00p							
5:30p							
6:00p							
6:30p							
7:00p							
7:30p							
8:00p							
8:30p							
9:00p							
9:30p							

	Revenues	Expenses	Profits
7DAY	$	$	$
YTD	$	$	$

Working (+):

Improve (-):

Daily Scoreboard	Mon	Tue	Wed	Thu	Fri	Sat	Sun

Top Priorities

#1	
#2	
#3	

✓ Professional Things To Do

✓	TP#	Next Best Action
	1	
	1	
	1	
	2	
	2	
	3	

✓ People I Want To Connect With This Week

✓ Things To Follow-Up On

Things For Later

Planning Parking From Desired Experiences

Progress Report, Wins, Celebrations, & Gratitude

My #1 focus for the month is...

% Done	25%	50%	75%	100%
Personal				
Career				
Money				
Family				
Social				
Health				
Spiritual				

Day	Breakfast	Lunch	Dinner
Mon			
Tue			
Wed			
Thu			
Fri			
Sat			
Sun			

Day	Weekend Ideas, Activities, & Intentions
Fri	
Sat	
Sun	

✓ Personal Things To Do

Notes

Tot hrs	Date / hrs	Date / hrs	Date / hrs	Date / hrs	Date / hrs	Date / hrs	Date / hrs
	Monday	**Tuesday**	**Wednesday**	**Thursday**	**Friday**	**Saturday**	**Sunday**
6:00a							
6:30a							
7:00a							
7:30a							
8:00a							
8:30a							
9:00a							
9:30a							
10:00a							
10:30a							
11:00a							
11:30a							
12:00p							
12:30p							
1:00p							
1:30p							
2:00p							
2:30p							
3:00p							
3:30p							
4:00p							
4:30p							
5:00p							
5:30p							
6:00p							
6:30p							
7:00p							
7:30p							
8:00p							
8:30p							
9:00p							
9:30p							

	Revenues	Expenses	Profits
7DAY	$	$	$
YTD	$	$	$

Working (+):

Improve (-):

Daily Scoreboard	Mon	Tue	Wed	Thu	Fri	Sat	Sun

Top Priorities

#1	
#2	
#3	

✓ Professional Things To Do

✓	TP#	Next Best Action
	1	
	1	
	1	
	2	
	2	
	3	

✓ People I Want To Connect With This Week

✓ Things To Follow-Up On

Things For Later

Planning Parking From Desired Experiences

Progress Report, Wins, Celebrations, & Gratitude

My #1 focus for the month is...

% Done	25%	50%	75%	100%
Personal				
Career				
Money				
Family				
Social				
Health				
Spiritual				

Day	Breakfast	Lunch	Dinner
Mon			
Tue			
Wed			
Thu			
Fri			
Sat			
Sun			

Day	Weekend Ideas, Activities, & Intentions
Fri	
Sat	
Sun	

✓ Personal Things To Do

Notes

Tot hrs	Date / hrs	Date / hrs	Date / hrs	Date / hrs	Date / hrs	Date / hrs	Date / hrs
	Monday	**Tuesday**	**Wednesday**	**Thursday**	**Friday**	**Saturday**	**Sunday**
6:00a							
6:30a							
7:00a							
7:30a							
8:00a							
8:30a							
9:00a							
9:30a							
10:00a							
10:30a							
11:00a							
11:30a							
12:00p							
12:30p							
1:00p							
1:30p							
2:00p							
2:30p							
3:00p							
3:30p							
4:00p							
4:30p							
5:00p							
5:30p							
6:00p							
6:30p							
7:00p							
7:30p							
8:00p							
8:30p							
9:00p							
9:30p							

	Revenues	Expenses	Profits
7DAY	$	$	$
YTD	$	$	$

Working (+):

Improve (-):

Daily Scoreboard	Mon	Tue	Wed	Thu	Fri	Sat	Sun

Top Priorities

#1	
#2	
#3	

✓ Professional Things To Do

✓	TP#	Next Best Action
	1	
	1	
	1	
	2	
	2	
	3	

✓ People I Want To Connect With This Week

✓ Things To Follow-Up On

Things For Later

Planning Parking From Desired Experiences

Progress Report, Wins, Celebrations, & Gratitude

My #1 focus for the month is...

% Done	25%	50%	75%	100%
Personal				
Career				
Money				
Family				
Social				
Health				
Spiritual				

Day	Breakfast	Lunch	Dinner
Mon			
Tue			
Wed			
Thu			
Fri			
Sat			
Sun			

Day	Weekend Ideas, Activities, & Intentions
Fri	
Sat	
Sun	

✓ Personal Things To Do

Notes

Tot hrs	Date / hrs	Date / hrs	Date / hrs	Date / hrs	Date / hrs	Date / hrs	Date / hrs
	Monday	**Tuesday**	**Wednesday**	**Thursday**	**Friday**	**Saturday**	**Sunday**
6:00a							
6:30a							
7:00a							
7:30a							
8:00a							
8:30a							
9:00a							
9:30a							
10:00a							
10:30a							
11:00a							
11:30a							
12:00p							
12:30p							
1:00p							
1:30p							
2:00p							
2:30p							
3:00p							
3:30p							
4:00p							
4:30p							
5:00p							
5:30p							
6:00p							
6:30p							
7:00p							
7:30p							
8:00p							
8:30p							
9:00p							
9:30p							

	Revenues	Expenses	Profits
7DAY	$	$	$
YTD	$	$	$

Working (+):

Improve (-):

Daily Scoreboard	Mon	Tue	Wed	Thu	Fri	Sat	Sun

Top Priorities

#1	
#2	
#3	

✓ Professional Things To Do

✓	TP#	Next Best Action
	1	
	1	
	1	
	2	
	2	
	3	

✓ People I Want To Connect With This Week

✓ Things To Follow-Up On

Things For Later

Planning Parking From Desired Experiences

Progress Report, Wins, Celebrations, & Gratitude

My #1 focus for the month is...

% Done	25%	50%	75%	100%
Personal				
Career				
Money				
Family				
Social				
Health				
Spiritual				

Day	Breakfast	Lunch	Dinner
Mon			
Tue			
Wed			
Thu			
Fri			
Sat			
Sun			

Day	Weekend Ideas, Activities, & Intentions
Fri	
Sat	
Sun	

✓ Personal Things To Do

Notes

Tot hrs	Date / hrs	Date / hrs	Date / hrs	Date / hrs	Date / hrs	Date / hrs	Date / hrs
	Monday	**Tuesday**	**Wednesday**	**Thursday**	**Friday**	**Saturday**	**Sunday**
6:00a							
6:30a							
7:00a							
7:30a							
8:00a							
8:30a							
9:00a							
9:30a							
10:00a							
10:30a							
11:00a							
11:30a							
12:00p							
12:30p							
1:00p							
1:30p							
2:00p							
2:30p							
3:00p							
3:30p							
4:00p							
4:30p							
5:00p							
5:30p							
6:00p							
6:30p							
7:00p							
7:30p							
8:00p							
8:30p							
9:00p							
9:30p							

	Revenues	Expenses	Profits
7DAY	$	$	$
YTD	$	$	$

Working (+):

Improve (-):

Daily Scoreboard	Mon	Tue	Wed	Thu	Fri	Sat	Sun

Top Priorities

#1	
#2	
#3	

✓ Professional Things To Do

✓	TP#	Next Best Action
	1	
	1	
	1	
	2	
	2	
	3	

✓ People I Want To Connect With This Week

✓ Things To Follow-Up On

Things For Later

Planning Parking From Desired Experiences

Progress Report, Wins, Celebrations, & Gratitude

My #1 focus for the month is...

% Done	25%	50%	75%	100%
Personal				
Career				
Money				
Family				
Social				
Health				
Spiritual				

Day	Breakfast	Lunch	Dinner
Mon			
Tue			
Wed			
Thu			
Fri			
Sat			
Sun			

Day	Weekend Ideas, Activities, & Intentions
Fri	
Sat	
Sun	

✓ Personal Things To Do

Notes

Tot **hrs**	Date /	**hrs**	Date /	**hrs**	Date /	**hrs**	Date /	**hrs**	Date /	**hrs**	Date /	**hrs**	Date /	**hrs**
	Monday		**Tuesday**		**Wednesday**		**Thursday**		**Friday**		**Saturday**		**Sunday**	
6:00a														
6:30a														
7:00a														
7:30a														
8:00a														
8:30a														
9:00a														
9:30a														
10:00a														
10:30a														
11:00a														
11:30a														
12:00p														
12:30p														
1:00p														
1:30p														
2:00p														
2:30p														
3:00p														
3:30p														
4:00p														
4:30p														
5:00p														
5:30p														
6:00p														
6:30p														
7:00p														
7:30p														
8:00p														
8:30p														
9:00p														
9:30p														

	Revenues	Expenses	Profits
7DAY	$	$	$
YTD	$	$	$

Working (+):

Improve (-):

Daily Scoreboard	Mon	Tue	Wed	Thu	Fri	Sat	Sun

Top Priorities

#1	
#2	
#3	

✓ Professional Things To Do

✓	TP#	Next Best Action
	1	
	1	
	1	
	2	
	2	
	3	

✓ People I Want To Connect With This Week

✓ Things To Follow-Up On

Things For Later

Planning Parking From Desired Experiences

Progress Report, Wins, Celebrations, & Gratitude

My #1 focus for the month is...

% Done	25%	50%	75%	100%
Personal				
Career				
Money				
Family				
Social				
Health				
Spiritual				

Day	Breakfast	Lunch	Dinner
Mon			
Tue			
Wed			
Thu			
Fri			
Sat			
Sun			

Day	Weekend Ideas, Activities, & Intentions
Fri	
Sat	
Sun	

✓ Personal Things To Do

Notes

Tot **hrs**	Date /	**hrs**	Date /	**hrs**	Date /	**hrs**	Date /	**hrs**	Date /	**hrs**	Date /	**hrs**	Date /	**hrs**
	Monday		**Tuesday**		**Wednesday**		**Thursday**		**Friday**		**Saturday**		**Sunday**	
6:00a														
6:30a														
7:00a														
7:30a														
8:00a														
8:30a														
9:00a														
9:30a														
10:00a														
10:30a														
11:00a														
11:30a														
12:00p														
12:30p														
1:00p														
1:30p														
2:00p														
2:30p														
3:00p														
3:30p														
4:00p														
4:30p														
5:00p														
5:30p														
6:00p														
6:30p														
7:00p														
7:30p														
8:00p														
8:30p														
9:00p														
9:30p														

1ST QUARTERLY

Personal

Describing How I Felt
Write three words that describe how you felt this quarter and explain why.

3 words: _____

Why? _____

_____

_____

New Choices Next Quarter
Write three new intentions for next quarter to make it even better than this one.

1. _____

2. _____

3. _____

Most Memorable & Meaningful Moments
List three moments from the quarter that you are grateful for.

1. _____

2. _____

3. _____

Monthly Checklist
Complete the following tasks before stepping into next quarter.

- ❑ Add important events onto my calendar
- ❑ Organize and clean my home & workspace
- ❑ Backup my computer files
- ❑ Calculate my quarterly cash flow

- ❑ _____
- ❑ _____
- ❑ _____
- ❑ _____

Profession

How Did You Or You Company Grow?
Explain how you and/or your company grew this quarter? Where is the momentum

_____

_____

_____

_____

_____

High Performance Habits
List behaviors that you did this quarter that helped you perform at a higher level.

_____

_____

_____

_____

_____

Low Performance Habits
List behaviors that you did this quarter that hindered your performance.

_____

_____

_____

_____

_____

	Revenues	Expenses	Profits
7DAY	$	$	$
YTD	$	$	$

Working (+):

Improve (-):

Daily Scoreboard	Mon	Tue	Wed	Thu	Fri	Sat	Sun

Top Priorities

#1	
#2	
#3	

✓ Professional Things To Do

✓	TP#	Next Best Action
	1	
	1	
	1	
	2	
	2	
	3	

✓ People I Want To Connect With This Week

✓ Things To Follow-Up On

Things For Later

Planning Parking From Desired Experiences

Progress Report, Wins, Celebrations, & Gratitude

My #1 focus for the month is...

% Done	25%	50%	75%	100%
Personal				
Career				
Money				
Family				
Social				
Health				
Spiritual				

Day	Breakfast	Lunch	Dinner
Mon			
Tue			
Wed			
Thu			
Fri			
Sat			
Sun			

Day	Weekend Ideas, Activities, & Intentions
Fri	
Sat	
Sun	

✓ Personal Things To Do

Notes

Tot **hrs**	Date / **hrs**	Date / **hrs**	Date / **hrs**	Date / **hrs**	Date / **hrs**	Date / **hrs**	Date / **hrs**
	Monday	**Tuesday**	**Wednesday**	**Thursday**	**Friday**	**Saturday**	**Sunday**
6:00a							
6:30a							
7:00a							
7:30a							
8:00a							
8:30a							
9:00a							
9:30a							
10:00a							
10:30a							
11:00a							
11:30a							
12:00p							
12:30p							
1:00p							
1:30p							
2:00p							
2:30p							
3:00p							
3:30p							
4:00p							
4:30p							
5:00p							
5:30p							
6:00p							
6:30p							
7:00p							
7:30p							
8:00p							
8:30p							
9:00p							
9:30p							

	Revenues	Expenses	Profits
7DAY	$	$	$
YTD	$	$	$

Working (+):

Improve (-):

Daily Scoreboard	Mon	Tue	Wed	Thu	Fri	Sat	Sun

Top Priorities

#1	
#2	
#3	

✓ Professional Things To Do

✓	TP#	Next Best Action
	1	
	1	
	1	
	2	
	2	
	3	

✓ People I Want To Connect With This Week

✓ Things To Follow-Up On

Things For Later

Planning Parking From Desired Experiences

Progress Report, Wins, Celebrations, & Gratitude

My #1 focus for the month is...

% Done	25%	50%	75%	100%
Personal				
Career				
Money				
Family				
Social				
Health				
Spiritual				

Day	Breakfast	Lunch	Dinner
Mon			
Tue			
Wed			
Thu			
Fri			
Sat			
Sun			

Day	Weekend Ideas, Activities, & Intentions
Fri	
Sat	
Sun	

✓ Personal Things To Do

Notes

Tot **hrs**	Date / **hrs**	Date / **hrs**	Date / **hrs**	Date / **hrs**	Date / **hrs**	Date / **hrs**	Date / **hrs**
	Monday	**Tuesday**	**Wednesday**	**Thursday**	**Friday**	**Saturday**	**Sunday**
6:00a							
6:30a							
7:00a							
7:30a							
8:00a							
8:30a							
9:00a							
9:30a							
10:00a							
10:30a							
11:00a							
11:30a							
12:00p							
12:30p							
1:00p							
1:30p							
2:00p							
2:30p							
3:00p							
3:30p							
4:00p							
4:30p							
5:00p							
5:30p							
6:00p							
6:30p							
7:00p							
7:30p							
8:00p							
8:30p							
9:00p							
9:30p							

	Revenues	Expenses	Profits
7DAY	$	$	$
YTD	$	$	$

Working (+):

Improve (-):

Daily Scoreboard	Mon	Tue	Wed	Thu	Fri	Sat	Sun

Top Priorities

#1	
#2	
#3	

✓ Professional Things To Do

✓	TP#	Next Best Action
	1	
	1	
	1	
	2	
	2	
	3	

✓ People I Want To Connect With This Week

✓ Things To Follow-Up On

Things For Later

Planning Parking From Desired Experiences

Progress Report, Wins, Celebrations, & Gratitude

My #1 focus for the month is...

% Done	25%	50%	75%	100%
Personal				
Career				
Money				
Family				
Social				
Health				
Spiritual				

Day	Breakfast	Lunch	Dinner
Mon			
Tue			
Wed			
Thu			
Fri			
Sat			
Sun			

Day	Weekend Ideas, Activities, & Intentions
Fri	
Sat	
Sun	

✓ Personal Things To Do

Notes

Tot **hrs**	Date / **hrs**	Date / **hrs**	Date / **hrs**	Date / **hrs**	Date / **hrs**	Date / **hrs**	Date / **hrs**
	Monday	**Tuesday**	**Wednesday**	**Thursday**	**Friday**	**Saturday**	**Sunday**
6:00a							
6:30a							
7:00a							
7:30a							
8:00a							
8:30a							
9:00a							
9:30a							
10:00a							
10:30a							
11:00a							
11:30a							
12:00p							
12:30p							
1:00p							
1:30p							
2:00p							
2:30p							
3:00p							
3:30p							
4:00p							
4:30p							
5:00p							
5:30p							
6:00p							
6:30p							
7:00p							
7:30p							
8:00p							
8:30p							
9:00p							
9:30p							

	Revenues	Expenses	Profits
7DAY	$	$	$
YTD	$	$	$

Working (+):

Improve (-):

Daily Scoreboard	Mon	Tue	Wed	Thu	Fri	Sat	Sun

Top Priorities

#1	
#2	
#3	

✓ Professional Things To Do

✓	TP#	Next Best Action
	1	
	1	
	1	
	2	
	2	
	3	

✓ People I Want To Connect With This Week

✓ Things To Follow-Up On

Things For Later

Planning Parking From Desired Experiences

Progress Report, Wins, Celebrations, & Gratitude

My #1 focus for the month is...

% Done	25%	50%	75%	100%
Personal				
Career				
Money				
Family				
Social				
Health				
Spiritual				

Day	Breakfast	Lunch	Dinner
Mon			
Tue			
Wed			
Thu			
Fri			
Sat			
Sun			

Day	Weekend Ideas, Activities, & Intentions
Fri	
Sat	
Sun	

✓ Personal Things To Do

Notes

	Monday	Tuesday	Wednesday	Thursday	Friday	Saturday	Sunday
6:00a							
6:30a							
7:00a							
7:30a							
8:00a							
8:30a							
9:00a							
9:30a							
10:00a							
10:30a							
11:00a							
11:30a							
12:00p							
12:30p							
1:00p							
1:30p							
2:00p							
2:30p							
3:00p							
3:30p							
4:00p							
4:30p							
5:00p							
5:30p							
6:00p							
6:30p							
7:00p							
7:30p							
8:00p							
8:30p							
9:00p							
9:30p							

	Revenues	Expenses	Profits
7DAY	$	$	$
YTD	$	$	$

Working (+):

Improve (-):

Daily Scoreboard	Mon	Tue	Wed	Thu	Fri	Sat	Sun

Top Priorities

#1	
#2	
#3	

✓ Professional Things To Do

✓	TP#	Next Best Action
	1	
	1	
	1	
	2	
	2	
	3	

✓ People I Want To Connect With This Week

✓	

✓ Things To Follow-Up On

✓	

Things For Later

Planning Parking From Desired Experiences

Progress Report, Wins, Celebrations, & Gratitude

My #1 focus for the month is...

% Done	25%	50%	75%	100%
Personal				
Career				
Money				
Family				
Social				
Health				
Spiritual				

Day	Breakfast	Lunch	Dinner
Mon			
Tue			
Wed			
Thu			
Fri			
Sat			
Sun			

Day	Weekend Ideas, Activities, & Intentions
Fri	
Sat	
Sun	

✓ Personal Things To Do

Notes

	Monday	Tuesday	Wednesday	Thursday	Friday	Saturday	Sunday
6:00a							
6:30a							
7:00a							
7:30a							
8:00a							
8:30a							
9:00a							
9:30a							
10:00a							
10:30a							
11:00a							
11:30a							
12:00p							
12:30p							
1:00p							
1:30p							
2:00p							
2:30p							
3:00p							
3:30p							
4:00p							
4:30p							
5:00p							
5:30p							
6:00p							
6:30p							
7:00p							
7:30p							
8:00p							
8:30p							
9:00p							
9:30p							

	Revenues	Expenses	Profits
7DAY	$	$	$
YTD	$	$	$

Working (+):

Improve (-):

Daily Scoreboard	Mon	Tue	Wed	Thu	Fri	Sat	Sun

Top Priorities

#1	
#2	
#3	

✓ Professional Things To Do

✓	TP#	Next Best Action
	1	
	1	
	1	
	2	
	2	
	3	

✓ People I Want To Connect With This Week

✓ Things To Follow-Up On

Things For Later

Planning Parking From Desired Experiences

Progress Report, Wins, Celebrations, & Gratitude

My #1 focus for the month is...

% Done	25% 50% 75% 100%
Personal	
Career	
Money	
Family	
Social	
Health	
Spiritual	

Day	Breakfast	Lunch	Dinner
Mon			
Tue			
Wed			
Thu			
Fri			
Sat			
Sun			

Day	Weekend Ideas, Activities, & Intentions
Fri	
Sat	
Sun	

✓ Personal Things To Do

Notes

Tot **hrs**	Date /	**hrs**	Date /	**hrs**	Date /	**hrs**	Date /	**hrs**	Date /	**hrs**	Date /	**hrs**	Date /	**hrs**
	Monday		**Tuesday**		**Wednesday**		**Thursday**		**Friday**		**Saturday**		**Sunday**	
6:00a														
6:30a														
7:00a														
7:30a														
8:00a														
8:30a														
9:00a														
9:30a														
10:00a														
10:30a														
11:00a														
11:30a														
12:00p														
12:30p														
1:00p														
1:30p														
2:00p														
2:30p														
3:00p														
3:30p														
4:00p														
4:30p														
5:00p														
5:30p														
6:00p														
6:30p														
7:00p														
7:30p														
8:00p														
8:30p														
9:00p	Date /	**hrs**	Date /	**hrs**	Date /	**hrs**	Date /	**hrs**	Date /	**hrs**	Date /	**hrs**	Date /	**hrs**
9:30p														

	Revenues	Expenses	Profits
7DAY	$	$	$
YTD	$	$	$

Working (+):

Improve (-):

Daily Scoreboard	Mon	Tue	Wed	Thu	Fri	Sat	Sun

Top Priorities

#1	
#2	
#3	

✓ Professional Things To Do

✓	TP#	Next Best Action
	1	
	1	
	1	
	2	
	2	
	3	

✓ People I Want To Connect With This Week

✓ Things To Follow-Up On

Things For Later

Planning Parking From Desired Experiences

Progress Report, Wins, Celebrations, & Gratitude

My #1 focus for the month is...

% Done	25%	50%	75%	100%
Personal				
Career				
Money				
Family				
Social				
Health				
Spiritual				

Day	Breakfast	Lunch	Dinner
Mon			
Tue			
Wed			
Thu			
Fri			
Sat			
Sun			

Day	Weekend Ideas, Activities, & Intentions
Fri	
Sat	
Sun	

✓ Personal Things To Do

Notes

Tot **hrs**	Date / **hrs**	Date / **hrs**	Date / **hrs**	Date / **hrs**	Date / **hrs**	Date / **hrs**	Date / **hrs**
	Monday	**Tuesday**	**Wednesday**	**Thursday**	**Friday**	**Saturday**	**Sunday**
6:00a							
6:30a							
7:00a							
7:30a							
8:00a							
8:30a							
9:00a							
9:30a							
10:00a							
10:30a							
11:00a							
11:30a							
12:00p							
12:30p							
1:00p							
1:30p							
2:00p							
2:30p							
3:00p							
3:30p							
4:00p							
4:30p							
5:00p							
5:30p							
6:00p							
6:30p							
7:00p							
7:30p							
8:00p							
8:30p							
9:00p							
9:30p							

	Revenues	Expenses	Profits
7DAY	$	$	$
YTD	$	$	$

Working (+):

Improve (-):

Daily Scoreboard	Mon	Tue	Wed	Thu	Fri	Sat	Sun

Top Priorities

#1	
#2	
#3	

✓ Professional Things To Do

✓	TP#	Next Best Action
	1	
	1	
	1	
	2	
	2	
	3	

✓ People I Want To Connect With This Week

✓ Things To Follow-Up On

Things For Later

Planning Parking From Desired Experiences

Progress Report, Wins, Celebrations, & Gratitude

My #1 focus for the month is...

% Done	25%	50%	75%	100%
Personal				
Career				
Money				
Family				
Social				
Health				
Spiritual				

Day	Breakfast	Lunch	Dinner
Mon			
Tue			
Wed			
Thu			
Fri			
Sat			
Sun			

Day	Weekend Ideas, Activities, & Intentions
Fri	
Sat	
Sun	

✓ Personal Things To Do

Notes

	Monday	Tuesday	Wednesday	Thursday	Friday	Saturday	Sunday
6:00a							
6:30a							
7:00a							
7:30a							
8:00a							
8:30a							
9:00a							
9:30a							
10:00a							
10:30a							
11:00a							
11:30a							
12:00p							
12:30p							
1:00p							
1:30p							
2:00p							
2:30p							
3:00p							
3:30p							
4:00p							
4:30p							
5:00p							
5:30p							
6:00p							
6:30p							
7:00p							
7:30p							
8:00p							
8:30p							
9:00p							
9:30p							

	Revenues	Expenses	Profits
7DAY	$	$	$
YTD	$	$	$

Working (+):

Improve (-):

Daily Scoreboard	Mon	Tue	Wed	Thu	Fri	Sat	Sun

Top Priorities

#1	
#2	
#3	

✓ Professional Things To Do

✓	TP#	Next Best Action
	1	
	1	
	1	
	2	
	2	
	3	

✓ People I Want To Connect With This Week

✓ Things To Follow-Up On

Things For Later

Planning Parking From Desired Experiences

Progress Report, Wins, Celebrations, & Gratitude

My #1 focus for the month is...

% Done	25%	50%	75%	100%
Personal				
Career				
Money				
Family				
Social				
Health				
Spiritual				

Day	Breakfast	Lunch	Dinner
Mon			
Tue			
Wed			
Thu			
Fri			
Sat			
Sun			

Day	Weekend Ideas, Activities, & Intentions
Fri	
Sat	
Sun	

✓ Personal Things To Do

Notes

Tot **hrs**	Date /	**hrs**	Date /	**hrs**	Date /	**hrs**	Date /	**hrs**	Date /	**hrs**	Date /	**hrs**	Date /	**hrs**
	Monday	**Tuesday**	**Wednesday**	**Thursday**	**Friday**	**Saturday**	**Sunday**
6:00a							
6:30a							
7:00a							
7:30a							
8:00a							
8:30a							
9:00a							
9:30a							
10:00a							
10:30a							
11:00a							
11:30a							
12:00p							
12:30p							
1:00p							
1:30p							
2:00p							
2:30p							
3:00p							
3:30p							
4:00p							
4:30p							
5:00p							
5:30p							
6:00p							
6:30p							
7:00p							
7:30p							
8:00p							
8:30p							
9:00p							
9:30p							

	Revenues	Expenses	Profits
7DAY	$	$	$
YTD	$	$	$

Working (+):

Improve (-):

Daily Scoreboard	Mon	Tue	Wed	Thu	Fri	Sat	Sun

Top Priorities

#1	
#2	
#3	

✓ Professional Things To Do

✓	TP#	Next Best Action
	1	
	1	
	1	
	2	
	2	
	3	

✓ People I Want To Connect With This Week

✓ Things To Follow-Up On

Things For Later

Planning Parking From Desired Experiences

Progress Report, Wins, Celebrations, & Gratitude

My #1 focus for the month is...

% Done	25%	50%	75%	100%
Personal				
Career				
Money				
Family				
Social				
Health				
Spiritual				

Day	Breakfast	Lunch	Dinner
Mon			
Tue			
Wed			
Thu			
Fri			
Sat			
Sun			

Day	Weekend Ideas, Activities, & Intentions
Fri	
Sat	
Sun	

✓ Personal Things To Do

Notes

Tot hrs	Date / hrs	Date / hrs	Date / hrs	Date / hrs	Date / hrs	Date / hrs	Date / hrs
	Monday	**Tuesday**	**Wednesday**	**Thursday**	**Friday**	**Saturday**	**Sunday**
6:00a							
6:30a							
7:00a							
7:30a							
8:00a							
8:30a							
9:00a							
9:30a							
10:00a							
10:30a							
11:00a							
11:30a							
12:00p							
12:30p							
1:00p							
1:30p							
2:00p							
2:30p							
3:00p							
3:30p							
4:00p							
4:30p							
5:00p							
5:30p							
6:00p							
6:30p							
7:00p							
7:30p							
8:00p							
8:30p							
9:00p							
9:30p							

	Revenues	Expenses	Profits
7DAY	$	$	$
YTD	$	$	$

Working (+):

Improve (-):

Daily Scoreboard	Mon	Tue	Wed	Thu	Fri	Sat	Sun

Top Priorities

#1	
#2	
#3	

✓	Professional Things To Do	

✓	TP#	Next Best Action
	1	
	1	
	1	
	2	
	2	
	3	

✓	People I Want To Connect With This Week

✓	Things To Follow-Up On

Things For Later

Planning Parking From Desired Experiences

Progress Report, Wins, Celebrations, & Gratitude

My #1 focus for the month is...

% Done	25%	50%	75%	100%
Personal				
Career				
Money				
Family				
Social				
Health				
Spiritual				

Day	Breakfast	Lunch	Dinner
Mon			
Tue			
Wed			
Thu			
Fri			
Sat			
Sun			

Day	Weekend Ideas, Activities, & Intentions
Fri	
Sat	
Sun	

✓	Personal Things To Do

Notes

	Monday	Tuesday	Wednesday	Thursday	Friday	Saturday	Sunday
6:00a							
6:30a							
7:00a							
7:30a							
8:00a							
8:30a							
9:00a							
9:30a							
10:00a							
10:30a							
11:00a							
11:30a							
12:00p							
12:30p							
1:00p							
1:30p							
2:00p							
2:30p							
3:00p							
3:30p							
4:00p							
4:30p							
5:00p							
5:30p							
6:00p							
6:30p							
7:00p							
7:30p							
8:00p							
8:30p							
9:00p							
9:30p							

	Revenues	Expenses	Profits
7DAY	$	$	$
YTD	$	$	$

Working (+):

Improve (-):

Daily Scoreboard	Mon	Tue	Wed	Thu	Fri	Sat	Sun

Top Priorities

#1	
#2	
#3	

✓ Professional Things To Do

✓	TP#	Next Best Action
	1	
	1	
	1	
	2	
	2	
	3	

✓ People I Want To Connect With This Week

✓ Things To Follow-Up On

Things For Later

Planning Parking From Desired Experiences

Progress Report, Wins, Celebrations, & Gratitude

My #1 focus for the month is...

% Done	25%	50%	75%	100%
Personal				
Career				
Money				
Family				
Social				
Health				
Spiritual				

Day	Breakfast	Lunch	Dinner
Mon			
Tue			
Wed			
Thu			
Fri			
Sat			
Sun			

Day	Weekend Ideas, Activities, & Intentions
Fri	
Sat	
Sun	

✓ Personal Things To Do

Notes

	Monday	Tuesday	Wednesday	Thursday	Friday	Saturday	Sunday
6:00a							
6:30a							
7:00a							
7:30a							
8:00a							
8:30a							
9:00a							
9:30a							
10:00a							
10:30a							
11:00a							
11:30a							
12:00p							
12:30p							
1:00p							
1:30p							
2:00p							
2:30p							
3:00p							
3:30p							
4:00p							
4:30p							
5:00p							
5:30p							
6:00p							
6:30p							
7:00p							
7:30p							
8:00p							
8:30p							
9:00p							
9:30p							

	Revenues	Expenses	Profits
7DAY	$	$	$
YTD	$	$	$

Working (+):

Improve (-):

Daily Scoreboard	Mon	Tue	Wed	Thu	Fri	Sat	Sun

Top Priorities

#1	
#2	
#3	

✓ Professional Things To Do

✓	TP#	Next Best Action
	1	
	1	
	1	
	2	
	2	
	3	

✓ People I Want To Connect With This Week

✓ Things To Follow-Up On

Things For Later

Planning Parking From Desired Experiences

Progress Report, Wins, Celebrations, & Gratitude

My #1 focus for the month is...

% Done	25%	50%	75%	100%
Personal				
Career				
Money				
Family				
Social				
Health				
Spiritual				

Day	Breakfast	Lunch	Dinner
Mon			
Tue			
Wed			
Thu			
Fri			
Sat			
Sun			

Day	Weekend Ideas, Activities, & Intentions
Fri	
Sat	
Sun	

✓ Personal Things To Do

Notes

Tot hrs	Date /	hrs	Date /	hrs	Date /	hrs	Date /	hrs	Date /	hrs	Date /	hrs	Date /	hrs
	Monday		Tuesday		Wednesday		Thursday		Friday		Saturday		Sunday	
6:00a														
6:30a														
7:00a														
7:30a														
8:00a														
8:30a														
9:00a														
9:30a														
10:00a														
10:30a														
11:00a														
11:30a														
12:00p														
12:30p														
1:00p														
1:30p														
2:00p														
2:30p														
3:00p														
3:30p														
4:00p														
4:30p														
5:00p														
5:30p														
6:00p														
6:30p														
7:00p														
7:30p														
8:00p														
8:30p														
9:00p														
9:30p														

2ND QUARTERLY

Personal

Describing How I Felt
Write three words that describe how you felt this quarter and explain why.

3 words: _____

Why? _____

_____

_____

New Choices Next Quarter
Write three new intentions for next quarter to make it even better than this one.

1. _____

2. _____

3. _____

Most Memorable & Meaningful Moments
List three moments from the quarter that you are grateful for.

1. _____

2. _____

3. _____

Monthly Checklist
Complete the following tasks before stepping into next quarter.

❏ Add important events onto my calendar   ❏ _____

❏ Organize and clean my home & workspace   ❏ _____

❏ Backup my computer files   ❏ _____

❏ Calculate my quarterly cash flow   ❏ _____

ASSESSMENT

Profession

How Did You Or You Company Grow?
Explain how you and/or your company grew this quarter? Where is the momentum

_____

_____

_____

_____

_____

_____

High Performance Habits
List behaviors that you did this quarter that helped you perform at a higher level.

_____

_____

_____

_____

_____

_____

Low Performance Habits
List behaviors that you did this quarter that hindered your performance.

_____

_____

_____

_____

_____

	Revenues	Expenses	Profits
7DAY	$	$	$
YTD	$	$	$

Working (+):

Improve (-):

Daily Scoreboard	Mon	Tue	Wed	Thu	Fri	Sat	Sun

Top Priorities

#1	
#2	
#3	

✓ Professional Things To Do

✓	TP#	Next Best Action
	1	
	1	
	1	
	2	
	2	
	3	

✓ People I Want To Connect With This Week

✓ Things To Follow-Up On

Things For Later

Planning Parking From Desired Experiences

Progress Report, Wins, Celebrations, & Gratitude

My #1 focus for the month is...

% Done	25%	50%	75%	100%
Personal				
Career				
Money				
Family				
Social				
Health				
Spiritual				

Day	Breakfast	Lunch	Dinner
Mon			
Tue			
Wed			
Thu			
Fri			
Sat			
Sun			

Day	Weekend Ideas, Activities, & Intentions
Fri	
Sat	
Sun	

✓ Personal Things To Do

Notes

Tot **hrs**	Date / **hrs**	Date / **hrs**	Date / **hrs**	Date / **hrs**	Date / **hrs**	Date / **hrs**	Date / **hrs**
	Monday	**Tuesday**	**Wednesday**	**Thursday**	**Friday**	**Saturday**	**Sunday**
6:00a							
6:30a							
7:00a							
7:30a							
8:00a							
8:30a							
9:00a							
9:30a							
10:00a							
10:30a							
11:00a							
11:30a							
12:00p							
12:30p							
1:00p							
1:30p							
2:00p							
2:30p							
3:00p							
3:30p							
4:00p							
4:30p							
5:00p							
5:30p							
6:00p							
6:30p							
7:00p							
7:30p							
8:00p							
8:30p							
9:00p							
9:30p							

	Revenues	Expenses	Profits
7DAY	$	$	$
YTD	$	$	$

Working (+):

Improve (-):

Daily Scoreboard	Mon	Tue	Wed	Thu	Fri	Sat	Sun

Top Priorities

#1	
#2	
#3	

✓ Professional Things To Do

✓	TP#	Next Best Action
	1	
	1	
	1	
	2	
	2	
	3	

✓ People I Want To Connect With This Week

✓ Things To Follow-Up On

Things For Later

Planning Parking From Desired Experiences

Progress Report, Wins, Celebrations, & Gratitude

My #1 focus for the month is...

% Done	25%	50%	75%	100%
Personal				
Career				
Money				
Family				
Social				
Health				
Spiritual				

Day	Breakfast	Lunch	Dinner
Mon			
Tue			
Wed			
Thu			
Fri			
Sat			
Sun			

Day	Weekend Ideas, Activities, & Intentions
Fri	
Sat	
Sun	

✓ Personal Things To Do

Notes

Tot hrs	Date / hrs	Date / hrs	Date / hrs	Date / hrs	Date / hrs	Date / hrs	Date / hrs
	Monday	**Tuesday**	**Wednesday**	**Thursday**	**Friday**	**Saturday**	**Sunday**
6:00a							
6:30a							
7:00a							
7:30a							
8:00a							
8:30a							
9:00a							
9:30a							
10:00a							
10:30a							
11:00a							
11:30a							
12:00p							
12:30p							
1:00p							
1:30p							
2:00p							
2:30p							
3:00p							
3:30p							
4:00p							
4:30p							
5:00p							
5:30p							
6:00p							
6:30p							
7:00p							
7:30p							
8:00p							
8:30p							
9:00p	Date / hrs	Date / hrs	Date / hrs	Date / hrs	Date / hrs	Date / hrs	Date / hrs
9:30p							

	Revenues	Expenses	Profits
7DAY	$	$	$
YTD	$	$	$

Working (+):

Improve (-):

Daily Scoreboard	Mon	Tue	Wed	Thu	Fri	Sat	Sun

Top Priorities

#1	
#2	
#3	

✓ Professional Things To Do

✓	TP#	Next Best Action
	1	
	1	
	1	
	2	
	2	
	3	

✓ People I Want To Connect With This Week

✓ Things To Follow-Up On

Things For Later

Planning Parking From Desired Experiences

Progress Report, Wins, Celebrations, & Gratitude

My #1 focus for the month is...

% Done	25%	50%	75%	100%
Personal				
Career				
Money				
Family				
Social				
Health				
Spiritual				

Day	Breakfast	Lunch	Dinner
Mon			
Tue			
Wed			
Thu			
Fri			
Sat			
Sun			

Day	Weekend Ideas, Activities, & Intentions
Fri	
Sat	
Sun	

✓ Personal Things To Do

Notes

Tot **hrs**	Date **/**	**hrs**	Date **/**	**hrs**	Date **/**	**hrs**	Date **/**	**hrs**	Date **/**	**hrs**	Date **/**	**hrs**	Date **/**	**hrs**
	Monday		**Tuesday**		**Wednesday**		**Thursday**		**Friday**		**Saturday**		**Sunday**	
6:00a														
6:30a														
7:00a														
7:30a														
8:00a														
8:30a														
9:00a														
9:30a														
10:00a														
10:30a														
11:00a														
11:30a														
12:00p														
12:30p														
1:00p														
1:30p														
2:00p														
2:30p														
3:00p														
3:30p														
4:00p														
4:30p														
5:00p														
5:30p														
6:00p														
6:30p														
7:00p														
7:30p														
8:00p														
8:30p														
9:00p														
9:30p														

	Revenues	Expenses	Profits
7DAY	$	$	$
YTD	$	$	$

Working (+):

Improve (-):

Daily Scoreboard	Mon	Tue	Wed	Thu	Fri	Sat	Sun

Top Priorities

#1	
#2	
#3	

✓ Professional Things To Do

✓	TP#	Next Best Action
	1	
	1	
	1	
	2	
	2	
	3	

✓ People I Want To Connect With This Week

✓ Things To Follow-Up On

Things For Later

Planning Parking From Desired Experiences

Progress Report, Wins, Celebrations, & Gratitude

My #1 focus for the month is...

% Done	25%	50%	75%	100%
Personal				
Career				
Money				
Family				
Social				
Health				
Spiritual				

Day	Breakfast	Lunch	Dinner
Mon			
Tue			
Wed			
Thu			
Fri			
Sat			
Sun			

Day	Weekend Ideas, Activities, & Intentions
Fri	
Sat	
Sun	

✓ Personal Things To Do

Notes

Tot hrs	Date / hrs	Date / hrs	Date / hrs	Date / hrs	Date / hrs	Date / hrs	Date / hrs
	Monday	**Tuesday**	**Wednesday**	**Thursday**	**Friday**	**Saturday**	**Sunday**
6:00a							
6:30a							
7:00a							
7:30a							
8:00a							
8:30a							
9:00a							
9:30a							
10:00a							
10:30a							
11:00a							
11:30a							
12:00p							
12:30p							
1:00p							
1:30p							
2:00p							
2:30p							
3:00p							
3:30p							
4:00p							
4:30p							
5:00p							
5:30p							
6:00p							
6:30p							
7:00p							
7:30p							
8:00p							
8:30p							
9:00p							
9:30p							

Revenues		Expenses		Profits	
7DAY	$		$		$
YTD	$		$		$

Working (+):

Improve (-):

Daily Scoreboard	Mon	Tue	Wed	Thu	Fri	Sat	Sun

Top Priorities

#1	
#2	
#3	

✓ Professional Things To Do

✓	TP#	Next Best Action
	1	
	1	
	1	
	2	
	2	
	3	

✓ People I Want To Connect With This Week

✓ Things To Follow-Up On

Things For Later

Planning Parking From Desired Experiences

Progress Report, Wins, Celebrations, & Gratitude

My #1 focus for the month is...

% Done	25%	50%	75%	100%
Personal				
Career				
Money				
Family				
Social				
Health				
Spiritual				

Day	Breakfast	Lunch	Dinner
Mon			
Tue			
Wed			
Thu			
Fri			
Sat			
Sun			

Day	Weekend Ideas, Activities, & Intentions
Fri	
Sat	
Sun	

✓ Personal Things To Do

Notes

Tot hrs	Date / hrs	Date / hrs	Date / hrs	Date / hrs	Date / hrs	Date / hrs	Date / hrs
	Monday	**Tuesday**	**Wednesday**	**Thursday**	**Friday**	**Saturday**	**Sunday**
6:00a							
6:30a							
7:00a							
7:30a							
8:00a							
8:30a							
9:00a							
9:30a							
10:00a							
10:30a							
11:00a							
11:30a							
12:00p							
12:30p							
1:00p							
1:30p							
2:00p							
2:30p							
3:00p							
3:30p							
4:00p							
4:30p							
5:00p							
5:30p							
6:00p							
6:30p							
7:00p							
7:30p							
8:00p							
8:30p							
9:00p							
9:30p							

	Revenues	Expenses	Profits
7DAY	$	$	$
YTD	$	$	$

Working (+):

Improve (-):

Daily Scoreboard	Mon	Tue	Wed	Thu	Fri	Sat	Sun

Top Priorities

#1	
#2	
#3	

✓ Professional Things To Do

✓	TP#	Next Best Action
	1	
	1	
	1	
	2	
	2	
	3	

✓ People I Want To Connect With This Week

✓ Things To Follow-Up On

Things For Later

Planning Parking From Desired Experiences

Progress Report, Wins, Celebrations, & Gratitude

My #1 focus for the month is...

% Done	25%	50%	75%	100%
Personal				
Career				
Money				
Family				
Social				
Health				
Spiritual				

Day	Breakfast	Lunch	Dinner
Mon			
Tue			
Wed			
Thu			
Fri			
Sat			
Sun			

Day	Weekend Ideas, Activities, & Intentions
Fri	
Sat	
Sun	

✓ Personal Things To Do

Notes

Tot hrs	Date / hrs	Date / hrs	Date / hrs	Date / hrs	Date / hrs	Date / hrs	Date / hrs
	Monday	**Tuesday**	**Wednesday**	**Thursday**	**Friday**	**Saturday**	**Sunday**
6:00a							
6:30a							
7:00a							
7:30a							
8:00a							
8:30a							
9:00a							
9:30a							
10:00a							
10:30a							
11:00a							
11:30a							
12:00p							
12:30p							
1:00p							
1:30p							
2:00p							
2:30p							
3:00p							
3:30p							
4:00p							
4:30p							
5:00p							
5:30p							
6:00p							
6:30p							
7:00p							
7:30p							
8:00p							
8:30p							
9:00p							
9:30p							

	Revenues	Expenses	Profits
7DAY	$	$	$
YTD	$	$	$

Working (+):

Improve (-):

Daily Scoreboard	Mon	Tue	Wed	Thu	Fri	Sat	Sun

Top Priorities

#1	
#2	
#3	

✓ Professional Things To Do

✓	TP#	Next Best Action
	1	
	1	
	1	
	2	
	2	
	3	

✓ People I Want To Connect With This Week

✓ Things To Follow-Up On

Things For Later

Planning Parking From Desired Experiences

Progress Report, Wins, Celebrations, & Gratitude

My #1 focus for the month is...

% Done	25%	50%	75%	100%
Personal				
Career				
Money				
Family				
Social				
Health				
Spiritual				

Day	Breakfast	Lunch	Dinner
Mon			
Tue			
Wed			
Thu			
Fri			
Sat			
Sun			

Day	Weekend Ideas, Activities, & Intentions
Fri	
Sat	
Sun	

✓ Personal Things To Do

Notes

Tot **hrs**	Date /	**hrs**	Date /	**hrs**	Date /	**hrs**	Date /	**hrs**	Date /	**hrs**	Date /	**hrs**	Date /	**hrs**
	Monday		**Tuesday**		**Wednesday**		**Thursday**		**Friday**		**Saturday**		**Sunday**	
6:00a														
6:30a														
7:00a														
7:30a														
8:00a														
8:30a														
9:00a														
9:30a														
10:00a														
10:30a														
11:00a														
11:30a														
12:00p														
12:30p														
1:00p														
1:30p														
2:00p														
2:30p														
3:00p														
3:30p														
4:00p														
4:30p														
5:00p														
5:30p														
6:00p														
6:30p														
7:00p														
7:30p														
8:00p														
8:30p														
9:00p														
9:30p														

	Revenues	Expenses	Profits
7DAY	$	$	$
YTD	$	$	$

Working (+):

Improve (-):

Daily Scoreboard	Mon	Tue	Wed	Thu	Fri	Sat	Sun

Top Priorities

#1	
#2	
#3	

✓	Professional Things To Do	

✓	TP#	Next Best Action
	1	
	1	
	1	
	2	
	2	
	3	

✓	People I Want To Connect With This Week

✓	Things To Follow-Up On

Things For Later

Planning Parking From Desired Experiences

Progress Report, Wins, Celebrations, & Gratitude

My #1 focus for the month is...

% Done	25%	50%	75%	100%
Personal				
Career				
Money				
Family				
Social				
Health				
Spiritual				

Day	Breakfast	Lunch	Dinner
Mon			
Tue			
Wed			
Thu			
Fri			
Sat			
Sun			

Day	Weekend Ideas, Activities, & Intentions
Fri	
Sat	
Sun	

✓	Personal Things To Do

Notes

Tot **hrs**	Date /	**hrs**	Date /	**hrs**	Date /	**hrs**	Date /	**hrs**	Date /	**hrs**	Date /	**hrs**	Date /	**hrs**
	Monday		**Tuesday**		**Wednesday**		**Thursday**		**Friday**		**Saturday**		**Sunday**	
6:00a														
6:30a														
7:00a														
7:30a														
8:00a														
8:30a														
9:00a														
9:30a														
10:00a														
10:30a														
11:00a														
11:30a														
12:00p														
12:30p														
1:00p														
1:30p														
2:00p														
2:30p														
3:00p														
3:30p														
4:00p														
4:30p														
5:00p														
5:30p														
6:00p														
6:30p														
7:00p														
7:30p														
8:00p														
8:30p														
9:00p														
9:30p														

	Revenues	Expenses	Profits
7DAY	$	$	$
YTD	$	$	$

Working (+):

Improve (-):

Daily Scoreboard	Mon	Tue	Wed	Thu	Fri	Sat	Sun

Top Priorities

#1	
#2	
#3	

✓ Professional Things To Do

✓	TP#	Next Best Action
	1	
	1	
	1	
	2	
	2	
	3	

✓ People I Want To Connect With This Week

✓ Things To Follow-Up On

Things For Later

Planning Parking From Desired Experiences

Progress Report, Wins, Celebrations, & Gratitude

My #1 focus for the month is...

% Done	25%	50%	75%	100%
Personal				
Career				
Money				
Family				
Social				
Health				
Spiritual				

Day	Breakfast	Lunch	Dinner
Mon			
Tue			
Wed			
Thu			
Fri			
Sat			
Sun			

Day	Weekend Ideas, Activities, & Intentions
Fri	
Sat	
Sun	

✓ Personal Things To Do

Notes

Tot **hrs**	Date / **hrs**	Date / **hrs**	Date / **hrs**	Date / **hrs**	Date / **hrs**	Date / **hrs**	Date / **hrs**
	Monday	**Tuesday**	**Wednesday**	**Thursday**	**Friday**	**Saturday**	**Sunday**
6:00a							
6:30a							
7:00a							
7:30a							
8:00a							
8:30a							
9:00a							
9:30a							
10:00a							
10:30a							
11:00a							
11:30a							
12:00p							
12:30p							
1:00p							
1:30p							
2:00p							
2:30p							
3:00p							
3:30p							
4:00p							
4:30p							
5:00p							
5:30p							
6:00p							
6:30p							
7:00p							
7:30p							
8:00p							
8:30p							
9:00p							
9:30p							

	Revenues	Expenses	Profits	
7DAY	$	$	$	
YTD	$	$	$	

Working (+):

Improve (-):

Daily Scoreboard	Mon	Tue	Wed	Thu	Fri	Sat	Sun

Top Priorities

#1	
#2	
#3	

✓ Professional Things To Do

✓	TP#	Next Best Action
	1	
	1	
	1	
	2	
	2	
	3	

✓ People I Want To Connect With This Week

✓ Things To Follow-Up On

Things For Later

Planning Parking From Desired Experiences

Progress Report, Wins, Celebrations, & Gratitude

My #1 focus for the month is...

% Done	25%	50%	75%	100%
Personal				
Career				
Money				
Family				
Social				
Health				
Spiritual				

Day	Breakfast	Lunch	Dinner
Mon			
Tue			
Wed			
Thu			
Fri			
Sat			
Sun			

Day	Weekend Ideas, Activities, & Intentions
Fri	
Sat	
Sun	

✓ Personal Things To Do

Notes

	Monday	Tuesday	Wednesday	Thursday	Friday	Saturday	Sunday
6:00a							
6:30a							
7:00a							
7:30a							
8:00a							
8:30a							
9:00a							
9:30a							
10:00a							
10:30a							
11:00a							
11:30a							
12:00p							
12:30p							
1:00p							
1:30p							
2:00p							
2:30p							
3:00p							
3:30p							
4:00p							
4:30p							
5:00p							
5:30p							
6:00p							
6:30p							
7:00p							
7:30p							
8:00p							
8:30p							
9:00p							
9:30p							

	Revenues	Expenses	Profits
7DAY	$	$	$
YTD	$	$	$

Working (+):

Improve (-):

Daily Scoreboard	Mon	Tue	Wed	Thu	Fri	Sat	Sun

Top Priorities

#1	
#2	
#3	

✓ Professional Things To Do

✓	TP#	Next Best Action
	1	
	1	
	1	
	2	
	2	
	3	

✓ People I Want To Connect With This Week

✓ Things To Follow-Up On

Things For Later

Planning Parking From Desired Experiences

Progress Report, Wins, Celebrations, & Gratitude

My #1 focus for the month is...

% Done	25%	50%	75%	100%
Personal				
Career				
Money				
Family				
Social				
Health				
Spiritual				

Day	Breakfast	Lunch	Dinner
Mon			
Tue			
Wed			
Thu			
Fri			
Sat			
Sun			

Day	Weekend Ideas, Activities, & Intentions
Fri	
Sat	
Sun	

✓ Personal Things To Do

Notes

Tot hrs	Date / hrs	Date / hrs	Date / hrs	Date / hrs	Date / hrs	Date / hrs	Date / hrs
	Monday	**Tuesday**	**Wednesday**	**Thursday**	**Friday**	**Saturday**	**Sunday**
6:00a							
6:30a							
7:00a							
7:30a							
8:00a							
8:30a							
9:00a							
9:30a							
10:00a							
10:30a							
11:00a							
11:30a							
12:00p							
12:30p							
1:00p							
1:30p							
2:00p							
2:30p							
3:00p							
3:30p							
4:00p							
4:30p							
5:00p							
5:30p							
6:00p							
6:30p							
7:00p							
7:30p							
8:00p							
8:30p							
9:00p							
9:30p							

	Revenues	Expenses	Profits
7DAY	$	$	$
YTD	$	$	$

Working (+):

Improve (-):

Daily Scoreboard	Mon	Tue	Wed	Thu	Fri	Sat	Sun

Top Priorities

#1	
#2	
#3	

✓ Professional Things To Do

✓	TP#	Next Best Action
	1	
	1	
	1	
	2	
	2	
	3	

✓ People I Want To Connect With This Week

✓ Things To Follow-Up On

Things For Later

Planning Parking From Desired Experiences

Progress Report, Wins, Celebrations, & Gratitude

My #1 focus for the month is...

% Done	25%	50%	75%	100%
Personal				
Career				
Money				
Family				
Social				
Health				
Spiritual				

Day	Breakfast	Lunch	Dinner
Mon			
Tue			
Wed			
Thu			
Fri			
Sat			
Sun			

Day	Weekend Ideas, Activities, & Intentions
Fri	
Sat	
Sun	

✓ Personal Things To Do

Notes

Tot **hrs**	Date / **hrs**	Date / **hrs**	Date / **hrs**	Date / **hrs**	Date / **hrs**	Date / **hrs**	Date / **hrs**
	Monday	**Tuesday**	**Wednesday**	**Thursday**	**Friday**	**Saturday**	**Sunday**
6:00a							
6:30a							
7:00a							
7:30a							
8:00a							
8:30a							
9:00a							
9:30a							
10:00a							
10:30a							
11:00a							
11:30a							
12:00p							
12:30p							
1:00p							
1:30p							
2:00p							
2:30p							
3:00p							
3:30p							
4:00p							
4:30p							
5:00p							
5:30p							
6:00p							
6:30p							
7:00p							
7:30p							
8:00p							
8:30p							
9:00p	Date / **hrs**	Date / **hrs**	Date / **hrs**	Date / **hrs**	Date / **hrs**	Date / **hrs**	Date / **hrs**
9:30p							

	Revenues	Expenses	Profits
7DAY	$	$	$
YTD	$	$	$

Working (+):

Improve (-):

Daily Scoreboard	Mon	Tue	Wed	Thu	Fri	Sat	Sun

Top Priorities

#1	
#2	
#3	

✓ Professional Things To Do

✓	TP#	Next Best Action
	1	
	1	
	1	
	2	
	2	
	3	

✓ People I Want To Connect With This Week

✓ Things To Follow-Up On

Things For Later

Planning Parking From Desired Experiences

Progress Report, Wins, Celebrations, & Gratitude

My #1 focus for the month is...

% Done	25%	50%	75%	100%
Personal				
Career				
Money				
Family				
Social				
Health				
Spiritual				

Day	Breakfast	Lunch	Dinner
Mon			
Tue			
Wed			
Thu			
Fri			
Sat			
Sun			

Day	Weekend Ideas, Activities, & Intentions
Fri	
Sat	
Sun	

✓ Personal Things To Do

Notes

Tot **hrs**	Date / **hrs**	Date / **hrs**	Date / **hrs**	Date / **hrs**	Date / **hrs**	Date / **hrs**	Date / **hrs**
	Monday	**Tuesday**	**Wednesday**	**Thursday**	**Friday**	**Saturday**	**Sunday**
6:00a							
6:30a							
7:00a							
7:30a							
8:00a							
8:30a							
9:00a							
9:30a							
10:00a							
10:30a							
11:00a							
11:30a							
12:00p							
12:30p							
1:00p							
1:30p							
2:00p							
2:30p							
3:00p							
3:30p							
4:00p							
4:30p							
5:00p							
5:30p							
6:00p							
6:30p							
7:00p							
7:30p							
8:00p							
8:30p							
9:00p							
9:30p							

3RD QUARTERLY

Personal

Describing How I Felt
Write three words that describe how you felt this quarter and explain why.

3 words: _____

Why? _____

_____

_____

New Choices Next Quarter
Write three new intentions for next quarter to make it even better than this one.

1. _____

2. _____

3. _____

Most Memorable & Meaningful Moments
List three moments from the quarter that you are grateful for.

1. _____

2. _____

3. _____

Monthly Checklist
Complete the following tasks before stepping into next quarter.

❏ Add important events onto my calendar   ❏ _____

❏ Organize and clean my home & workspace   ❏ _____

❏ Backup my computer files   ❏ _____

❏ Calculate my quarterly cash flow   ❏ _____

Profession

How Did You Or You Company Grow?
Explain how you and/or your company grew this quarter? Where is the momentum

_____

_____

_____

_____

_____

_____

High Performance Habits
List behaviors that you did this quarter that helped you perform at a higher level.

_____

_____

_____

_____

_____

_____

Low Performance Habits
List behaviors that you did this quarter that hindered your performance.

_____

_____

_____

_____

_____

	Revenues	Expenses	Profits
7DAY	$	$	$
YTD	$	$	$

Working (+):

Improve (-):

Daily Scoreboard	Mon	Tue	Wed	Thu	Fri	Sat	Sun

Top Priorities

#1	
#2	
#3	

✓ Professional Things To Do

✓	TP#	Next Best Action
	1	
	1	
	1	
	2	
	2	
	3	

✓ People I Want To Connect With This Week

✓ Things To Follow-Up On

Things For Later

Planning Parking From Desired Experiences

Progress Report, Wins, Celebrations, & Gratitude

My #1 focus for the month is...

% Done	25%	50%	75%	100%
Personal				
Career				
Money				
Family				
Social				
Health				
Spiritual				

Day	Breakfast	Lunch	Dinner
Mon			
Tue			
Wed			
Thu			
Fri			
Sat			
Sun			

Day	Weekend Ideas, Activities, & Intentions
Fri	
Sat	
Sun	

✓ Personal Things To Do

Notes

Tot **hrs**	Date **/** **hrs**	Date **/** **hrs**	Date **/** **hrs**	Date **/** **hrs**	Date **/** **hrs**	Date **/** **hrs**	Date **/** **hrs**
	Monday	**Tuesday**	**Wednesday**	**Thursday**	**Friday**	**Saturday**	**Sunday**
6:00a							
6:30a							
7:00a							
7:30a							
8:00a							
8:30a							
9:00a							
9:30a							
10:00a							
10:30a							
11:00a							
11:30a							
12:00p							
12:30p							
1:00p							
1:30p							
2:00p							
2:30p							
3:00p							
3:30p							
4:00p							
4:30p							
5:00p							
5:30p							
6:00p							
6:30p							
7:00p							
7:30p							
8:00p							
8:30p							
9:00p							
9:30p							

	Revenues	Expenses	Profits
7DAY	$	$	$
YTD	$	$	$

Working (+):

Improve (-):

Daily Scoreboard	Mon	Tue	Wed	Thu	Fri	Sat	Sun

Top Priorities

#1	
#2	
#3	

✓ Professional Things To Do

✓	TP#	Next Best Action
	1	
	1	
	1	
	2	
	2	
	3	

✓ People I Want To Connect With This Week

✓ Things To Follow-Up On

Things For Later

Planning Parking From Desired Experiences

Progress Report, Wins, Celebrations, & Gratitude

My #1 focus for the month is...

% Done	25%	50%	75%	100%
Personal				
Career				
Money				
Family				
Social				
Health				
Spiritual				

Day	Breakfast	Lunch	Dinner
Mon			
Tue			
Wed			
Thu			
Fri			
Sat			
Sun			

Day	Weekend Ideas, Activities, & Intentions
Fri	
Sat	
Sun	

✓ Personal Things To Do

Notes

Tot **hrs**	Date /	**hrs**	Date /	**hrs**	Date /	**hrs**	Date /	**hrs**	Date /	**hrs**	Date /	**hrs**	Date /	**hrs**
	Monday		**Tuesday**		**Wednesday**		**Thursday**		**Friday**		**Saturday**		**Sunday**	
6:00a														
6:30a														
7:00a														
7:30a														
8:00a														
8:30a														
9:00a														
9:30a														
10:00a														
10:30a														
11:00a														
11:30a														
12:00p														
12:30p														
1:00p														
1:30p														
2:00p														
2:30p														
3:00p														
3:30p														
4:00p														
4:30p														
5:00p														
5:30p														
6:00p														
6:30p														
7:00p														
7:30p														
8:00p														
8:30p														
9:00p														
9:30p														

	Revenues	Expenses	Profits
7DAY	$	$	$
YTD	$	$	$

Working (+):

Improve (-):

Daily Scoreboard	Mon	Tue	Wed	Thu	Fri	Sat	Sun

Top Priorities

#1	
#2	
#3	

✓ Professional Things To Do

✓	TP#	Next Best Action
	1	
	1	
	1	
	2	
	2	
	3	

✓ People I Want To Connect With This Week

✓ Things To Follow-Up On

Things For Later

Planning Parking From Desired Experiences

Progress Report, Wins, Celebrations, & Gratitude

My #1 focus for the month is...

% Done	25%	50%	75%	100%
Personal				
Career				
Money				
Family				
Social				
Health				
Spiritual				

Day	Breakfast	Lunch	Dinner
Mon			
Tue			
Wed			
Thu			
Fri			
Sat			
Sun			

Day	Weekend Ideas, Activities, & Intentions
Fri	
Sat	
Sun	

✓ Personal Things To Do

Notes

Tot **hrs**	Date / **hrs**	Date / **hrs**	Date / **hrs**	Date / **hrs**	Date / **hrs**	Date / **hrs**	Date / **hrs**
	Monday	**Tuesday**	**Wednesday**	**Thursday**	**Friday**	**Saturday**	**Sunday**
6:00a							
6:30a							
7:00a							
7:30a							
8:00a							
8:30a							
9:00a							
9:30a							
10:00a							
10:30a							
11:00a							
11:30a							
12:00p							
12:30p							
1:00p							
1:30p							
2:00p							
2:30p							
3:00p							
3:30p							
4:00p							
4:30p							
5:00p							
5:30p							
6:00p							
6:30p							
7:00p							
7:30p							
8:00p							
8:30p							
9:00p							
9:30p							

	Revenues	Expenses	Profits
7DAY	$	$	$
YTD	$	$	$

Working (+):

Improve (-):

Daily Scoreboard	Mon	Tue	Wed	Thu	Fri	Sat	Sun

Top Priorities

#1	
#2	
#3	

✓ Professional Things To Do

✓	TP#	Next Best Action
	1	
	1	
	1	
	2	
	2	
	3	

✓ People I Want To Connect With This Week

✓ Things To Follow-Up On

Things For Later

Planning Parking From Desired Experiences

Progress Report, Wins, Celebrations, & Gratitude

My #1 focus for the month is...

% Done	25%	50%	75%	100%
Personal				
Career				
Money				
Family				
Social				
Health				
Spiritual				

Day	Breakfast	Lunch	Dinner
Mon			
Tue			
Wed			
Thu			
Fri			
Sat			
Sun			

Day — Weekend Ideas, Activities, & Intentions

Fri	
Sat	
Sun	

✓ Personal Things To Do

Notes

Tot **hrs**	Date /	**hrs**	Date /	**hrs**	Date /	**hrs**	Date /	**hrs**	Date /	**hrs**	Date /	**hrs**	Date /	**hrs**
	Monday		**Tuesday**		**Wednesday**		**Thursday**		**Friday**		**Saturday**		**Sunday**	
6:00a														
6:30a														
7:00a														
7:30a														
8:00a														
8:30a														
9:00a														
9:30a														
10:00a														
10:30a														
11:00a														
11:30a														
12:00p														
12:30p														
1:00p														
1:30p														
2:00p														
2:30p														
3:00p														
3:30p														
4:00p														
4:30p														
5:00p														
5:30p														
6:00p														
6:30p														
7:00p														
7:30p														
8:00p														
8:30p														
9:00p														
9:30p														

	Revenues	Expenses	Profits
7DAY	$	$	$
YTD	$	$	$

Working (+):

Improve (-):

Daily Scoreboard	Mon	Tue	Wed	Thu	Fri	Sat	Sun

Top Priorities

#1	
#2	
#3	

✓ Professional Things To Do

✓	TP#	Next Best Action
	1	
	1	
	1	
	2	
	2	
	3	

✓ People I Want To Connect With This Week

✓ Things To Follow-Up On

Things For Later

Planning Parking From Desired Experiences

Progress Report, Wins, Celebrations, & Gratitude

My #1 focus for the month is...

% Done	25%	50%	75%	100%
Personal				
Career				
Money				
Family				
Social				
Health				
Spiritual				

Day	Breakfast	Lunch	Dinner
Mon			
Tue			
Wed			
Thu			
Fri			
Sat			
Sun			

Day	Weekend Ideas, Activities, & Intentions
Fri	
Sat	
Sun	

✓ Personal Things To Do

Notes

Tot **hrs**	Date / **hrs**	Date / **hrs**	Date / **hrs**	Date / **hrs**	Date / **hrs**	Date / **hrs**	Date / **hrs**
	Monday	**Tuesday**	**Wednesday**	**Thursday**	**Friday**	**Saturday**	**Sunday**
6:00a							
6:30a							
7:00a							
7:30a							
8:00a							
8:30a							
9:00a							
9:30a							
10:00a							
10:30a							
11:00a							
11:30a							
12:00p							
12:30p							
1:00p							
1:30p							
2:00p							
2:30p							
3:00p							
3:30p							
4:00p							
4:30p							
5:00p							
5:30p							
6:00p							
6:30p							
7:00p							
7:30p							
8:00p							
8:30p							
9:00p							
9:30p							

	Revenues	Expenses	Profits
7DAY	$	$	$
YTD	$	$	$

Working (+):

Improve (-):

Daily Scoreboard	Mon	Tue	Wed	Thu	Fri	Sat	Sun

Top Priorities

#1	
#2	
#3	

✓ Professional Things To Do

✓	TP#	Next Best Action
	1	
	1	
	1	
	2	
	2	
	3	

✓ People I Want To Connect With This Week

✓ Things To Follow-Up On

Things For Later

Planning Parking From Desired Experiences

Progress Report, Wins, Celebrations, & Gratitude

My #1 focus for the month is...

% Done	25%	50%	75%	100%
Personal				
Career				
Money				
Family				
Social				
Health				
Spiritual				

Day	Breakfast	Lunch	Dinner
Mon			
Tue			
Wed			
Thu			
Fri			
Sat			
Sun			

Day	Weekend Ideas, Activities, & Intentions
Fri	
Sat	
Sun	

✓ Personal Things To Do

Notes

Tot **hrs**	Date / **hrs**	Date / **hrs**	Date / **hrs**	Date / **hrs**	Date / **hrs**	Date / **hrs**	Date / **hrs**
	Monday	Tuesday	Wednesday	Thursday	Friday	Saturday	Sunday
6:00a							
6:30a							
7:00a							
7:30a							
8:00a							
8:30a							
9:00a							
9:30a							
10:00a							
10:30a							
11:00a							
11:30a							
12:00p							
12:30p							
1:00p							
1:30p							
2:00p							
2:30p							
3:00p							
3:30p							
4:00p							
4:30p							
5:00p							
5:30p							
6:00p							
6:30p							
7:00p							
7:30p							
8:00p							
8:30p							
9:00p							
9:30p							

	Revenues	Expenses	Profits
7DAY	$	$	$
YTD	$	$	$

Working (+):

Improve (-):

Daily Scoreboard	Mon	Tue	Wed	Thu	Fri	Sat	Sun

Top Priorities

#1	
#2	
#3	

✓ Professional Things To Do

✓	TP#	Next Best Action
	1	
	1	
	1	
	2	
	2	
	3	

✓ People I Want To Connect With This Week

✓ Things To Follow-Up On

Things For Later

Planning Parking From Desired Experiences

Progress Report, Wins, Celebrations, & Gratitude

My #1 focus for the month is...

% Done	25%	50%	75%	100%
Personal				
Career				
Money				
Family				
Social				
Health				
Spiritual				

Day	Breakfast	Lunch	Dinner
Mon			
Tue			
Wed			
Thu			
Fri			
Sat			
Sun			

Day	Weekend Ideas, Activities, & Intentions
Fri	
Sat	
Sun	

✓ Personal Things To Do

Notes

Tot **hrs**	Date /	**hrs**	Date /	**hrs**	Date /	**hrs**	Date /	**hrs**	Date /	**hrs**	Date /	**hrs**	Date /	**hrs**
	Monday	**Tuesday**	**Wednesday**	**Thursday**	**Friday**	**Saturday**	**Sunday**							
6:00a														
6:30a														
7:00a														
7:30a														
8:00a														
8:30a														
9:00a														
9:30a														
10:00a														
10:30a														
11:00a														
11:30a														
12:00p														
12:30p														
1:00p														
1:30p														
2:00p														
2:30p														
3:00p														
3:30p														
4:00p														
4:30p														
5:00p														
5:30p														
6:00p														
6:30p														
7:00p														
7:30p														
8:00p														
8:30p														
9:00p														
9:30p														

	Revenues	Expenses	Profits
7DAY	$	$	$
YTD	$	$	$

Working (+):

Improve (-):

Daily Scoreboard	Mon	Tue	Wed	Thu	Fri	Sat	Sun

Top Priorities

#1	
#2	
#3	

✓ Professional Things To Do

✓	TP#	Next Best Action
	1	
	1	
	1	
	2	
	2	
	3	

✓ People I Want To Connect With This Week

✓ Things To Follow-Up On

Things For Later

Planning Parking From Desired Experiences

Progress Report, Wins, Celebrations, & Gratitude

My #1 focus for the month is...

% Done	25%	50%	75%	100%
Personal				
Career				
Money				
Family				
Social				
Health				
Spiritual				

Day	Breakfast	Lunch	Dinner
Mon			
Tue			
Wed			
Thu			
Fri			
Sat			
Sun			

Day	Weekend Ideas, Activities, & Intentions
Fri	
Sat	
Sun	

✓ Personal Things To Do

Notes

Tot **hrs**	Date / **hrs**	Date / **hrs**	Date / **hrs**	Date / **hrs**	Date / **hrs**	Date / **hrs**	Date / **hrs**
	Monday	**Tuesday**	**Wednesday**	**Thursday**	**Friday**	**Saturday**	**Sunday**
6:00a							
6:30a							
7:00a							
7:30a							
8:00a							
8:30a							
9:00a							
9:30a							
10:00a							
10:30a							
11:00a							
11:30a							
12:00p							
12:30p							
1:00p							
1:30p							
2:00p							
2:30p							
3:00p							
3:30p							
4:00p							
4:30p							
5:00p							
5:30p							
6:00p							
6:30p							
7:00p							
7:30p							
8:00p							
8:30p							
9:00p							
9:30p							

	Revenues	Expenses	Profits
7DAY	$	$	$
YTD	$	$	$

Working (+):

Improve (-):

Daily Scoreboard	Mon	Tue	Wed	Thu	Fri	Sat	Sun

Top Priorities

#1	
#2	
#3	

✓ Professional Things To Do

✓	TP#	Next Best Action
	1	
	1	
	1	
	2	
	2	
	3	

✓ People I Want To Connect With This Week

✓ Things To Follow-Up On

Things For Later

Planning Parking From Desired Experiences

Progress Report, Wins, Celebrations, & Gratitude

My #1 focus for the month is...

% Done	25%	50%	75%	100%
Personal				
Career				
Money				
Family				
Social				
Health				
Spiritual				

Day	Breakfast	Lunch	Dinner
Mon			
Tue			
Wed			
Thu			
Fri			
Sat			
Sun			

Day	Weekend Ideas, Activities, & Intentions
Fri	
Sat	
Sun	

✓ Personal Things To Do

Notes

Tot **hrs**	Date /	**hrs**	Date /	**hrs**	Date /	**hrs**	Date /	**hrs**	Date /	**hrs**	Date /	**hrs**	Date /	**hrs**
	Monday	**Tuesday**	**Wednesday**	**Thursday**	**Friday**	**Saturday**	**Sunday**							
6:00a														
6:30a														
7:00a														
7:30a														
8:00a														
8:30a														
9:00a														
9:30a														
10:00a														
10:30a														
11:00a														
11:30a														
12:00p														
12:30p														
1:00p														
1:30p														
2:00p														
2:30p														
3:00p														
3:30p														
4:00p														
4:30p														
5:00p														
5:30p														
6:00p														
6:30p														
7:00p														
7:30p														
8:00p														
8:30p														
9:00p														
9:30p														

	Revenues	Expenses	Profits
7DAY	$	$	$
YTD	$	$	$

Working (+):

Improve (-):

Daily Scoreboard	Mon	Tue	Wed	Thu	Fri	Sat	Sun

Top Priorities

#1	
#2	
#3	

✓ Professional Things To Do

✓	TP#	Next Best Action
	1	
	1	
	1	
	2	
	2	
	3	

✓ People I Want To Connect With This Week

✓ Things To Follow-Up On

Things For Later

Planning Parking From Desired Experiences

Progress Report, Wins, Celebrations, & Gratitude

My #1 focus for the month is...

% Done	25%	50%	75%	100%
Personal				
Career				
Money				
Family				
Social				
Health				
Spiritual				

Day	Breakfast	Lunch	Dinner
Mon			
Tue			
Wed			
Thu			
Fri			
Sat			
Sun			

Day	Weekend Ideas, Activities, & Intentions
Fri	
Sat	
Sun	

✓ Personal Things To Do

Notes

Tot hrs	Date / hrs	Date / hrs	Date / hrs	Date / hrs	Date / hrs	Date / hrs	Date / hrs
	Monday	Tuesday	Wednesday	Thursday	Friday	Saturday	Sunday
6:00a							
6:30a							
7:00a							
7:30a							
8:00a							
8:30a							
9:00a							
9:30a							
10:00a							
10:30a							
11:00a							
11:30a							
12:00p							
12:30p							
1:00p							
1:30p							
2:00p							
2:30p							
3:00p							
3:30p							
4:00p							
4:30p							
5:00p							
5:30p							
6:00p							
6:30p							
7:00p							
7:30p							
8:00p							
8:30p							
9:00p							
9:30p							

	Revenues	Expenses	Profits
7DAY	$	$	$
YTD	$	$	$

Working (+):

Improve (-):

Daily Scoreboard	Mon	Tue	Wed	Thu	Fri	Sat	Sun

Top Priorities

#1	
#2	
#3	

✓ Professional Things To Do

✓	TP#	Next Best Action
	1	
	1	
	1	
	2	
	2	
	3	

✓ People I Want To Connect With This Week

✓ Things To Follow-Up On

Things For Later

Planning Parking From Desired Experiences

Progress Report, Wins, Celebrations, & Gratitude

My #1 focus for the month is...

% Done	25%	50%	75%	100%
Personal				
Career				
Money				
Family				
Social				
Health				
Spiritual				

Day	Breakfast	Lunch	Dinner
Mon			
Tue			
Wed			
Thu			
Fri			
Sat			
Sun			

Day	Weekend Ideas, Activities, & Intentions
Fri	
Sat	
Sun	

✓ Personal Things To Do

Notes

Tot **hrs**	Date **/**	**hrs**	Date **/**	**hrs**	Date **/**	**hrs**	Date **/**	**hrs**	Date **/**	**hrs**	Date **/**	**hrs**	Date **/**	**hrs**
	Monday		**Tuesday**		**Wednesday**		**Thursday**		**Friday**		**Saturday**		**Sunday**	
6:00a														
6:30a														
7:00a														
7:30a														
8:00a														
8:30a														
9:00a														
9:30a														
10:00a														
10:30a														
11:00a														
11:30a														
12:00p														
12:30p														
1:00p														
1:30p														
2:00p														
2:30p														
3:00p														
3:30p														
4:00p														
4:30p														
5:00p														
5:30p														
6:00p														
6:30p														
7:00p														
7:30p														
8:00p														
8:30p														
9:00p														
9:30p														

	Revenues	Expenses	Profits
7DAY	$	$	$
YTD	$	$	$

Working (+):

Improve (-):

Daily Scoreboard	Mon	Tue	Wed	Thu	Fri	Sat	Sun

Top Priorities

#1	
#2	
#3	

✓ Professional Things To Do

✓	TP#	Next Best Action
	1	
	1	
	1	
	2	
	2	
	3	

✓ People I Want To Connect With This Week

✓ Things To Follow-Up On

Things For Later

Planning Parking From Desired Experiences

Progress Report, Wins, Celebrations, & Gratitude

My #1 focus for the month is...

% Done	25%	50%	75%	100%
Personal				
Career				
Money				
Family				
Social				
Health				
Spiritual				

Day	Breakfast	Lunch	Dinner
Mon			
Tue			
Wed			
Thu			
Fri			
Sat			
Sun			

Day	Weekend Ideas, Activities, & Intentions
Fri	
Sat	
Sun	

✓ Personal Things To Do

Notes

Tot **hrs**	Date **/**	**hrs**	Date **/**	**hrs**	Date **/**	**hrs**	Date **/**	**hrs**	Date **/**	**hrs**	Date **/**	**hrs**	Date **/**	**hrs**
	Monday		**Tuesday**		**Wednesday**		**Thursday**		**Friday**		**Saturday**		**Sunday**	
6:00a														
6:30a														
7:00a														
7:30a														
8:00a														
8:30a														
9:00a														
9:30a														
10:00a														
10:30a														
11:00a														
11:30a														
12:00p														
12:30p														
1:00p														
1:30p														
2:00p														
2:30p														
3:00p														
3:30p														
4:00p														
4:30p														
5:00p														
5:30p														
6:00p														
6:30p														
7:00p														
7:30p														
8:00p														
8:30p														
9:00p														
9:30p														

	Revenues	Expenses	Profits
7DAY	$	$	$
YTD	$	$	$

Working (+):

Improve (-):

Daily Scoreboard	Mon	Tue	Wed	Thu	Fri	Sat	Sun

Top Priorities

#1	
#2	
#3	

✓ Professional Things To Do

✓	TP#	Next Best Action
	1	
	1	
	1	
	2	
	2	
	3	

✓ People I Want To Connect With This Week

✓ Things To Follow-Up On

Things For Later

Planning Parking From Desired Experiences

Progress Report, Wins, Celebrations, & Gratitude

My #1 focus for the month is...

% Done	25%	50%	75%	100%
Personal				
Career				
Money				
Family				
Social				
Health				
Spiritual				

Day	Breakfast	Lunch	Dinner
Mon			
Tue			
Wed			
Thu			
Fri			
Sat			
Sun			

Day	Weekend Ideas, Activities, & Intentions
Fri	
Sat	
Sun	

✓ Personal Things To Do

Notes

Tot hrs	Date / hrs	Date / hrs	Date / hrs	Date / hrs	Date / hrs	Date / hrs	Date / hrs
	Monday	Tuesday	Wednesday	Thursday	Friday	Saturday	Sunday
6:00a							
6:30a							
7:00a							
7:30a							
8:00a							
8:30a							
9:00a							
9:30a							
10:00a							
10:30a							
11:00a							
11:30a							
12:00p							
12:30p							
1:00p							
1:30p							
2:00p							
2:30p							
3:00p							
3:30p							
4:00p							
4:30p							
5:00p							
5:30p							
6:00p							
6:30p							
7:00p							
7:30p							
8:00p							
8:30p							
9:00p							
9:30p							

	Revenues	Expenses	Profits
7DAY	$	$	$
YTD	$	$	$

Working (+):

Improve (-):

Daily Scoreboard	Mon	Tue	Wed	Thu	Fri	Sat	Sun

Top Priorities

#1	
#2	
#3	

✓ Professional Things To Do

✓	TP#	Next Best Action
	1	
	1	
	1	
	2	
	2	
	3	

✓ People I Want To Connect With This Week

✓ Things To Follow-Up On

Things For Later

Planning Parking From Desired Experiences

Progress Report, Wins, Celebrations, & Gratitude

My #1 focus for the month is...

% Done	25%	50%	75%	100%
Personal				
Career				
Money				
Family				
Social				
Health				
Spiritual				

Day	Breakfast	Lunch	Dinner
Mon			
Tue			
Wed			
Thu			
Fri			
Sat			
Sun			

Day	Weekend Ideas, Activities, & Intentions
Fri	
Sat	
Sun	

✓ Personal Things To Do

Notes

Tot **hrs**	Date / **hrs**	Date / **hrs**	Date / **hrs**	Date / **hrs**	Date / **hrs**	Date / **hrs**	Date / **hrs**
	Monday	**Tuesday**	**Wednesday**	**Thursday**	**Friday**	**Saturday**	**Sunday**
6:00a							
6:30a							
7:00a							
7:30a							
8:00a							
8:30a							
9:00a							
9:30a							
10:00a							
10:30a							
11:00a							
11:30a							
12:00p							
12:30p							
1:00p							
1:30p							
2:00p							
2:30p							
3:00p							
3:30p							
4:00p							
4:30p							
5:00p							
5:30p							
6:00p							
6:30p							
7:00p							
7:30p							
8:00p							
8:30p							
9:00p							
9:30p							

4TH QUARTERLY

Personal

Describing How I Felt
Write three words that describe how you felt this quarter and explain why.

3 words: _____

Why? _____

_____

_____

New Choices Next Quarter
Write three new intentions for next quarter to make it even better than this one.

1. _____

2. _____

3. _____

Most Memorable & Meaningful Moments
List three moments from the quarter that you are grateful for.

1. _____

2. _____

3. _____

Monthly Checklist
Complete the following tasks before stepping into next quarter.

❐ Add important events onto my calendar ❐ _____

❐ Organize and clean my home & workspace ❐ _____

❐ Backup my computer files ❐ _____

❐ Calculate my quarterly cash flow ❐ _____

ASSESSMENT

How Did You Or You Company Grow?

Explain how you and/or your company grew this quarter? Where is the momentum?

High Performance Habits

List behaviors that you did this quarter that helped you perform at a higher level.

Low Performance Habits

List behaviors that you did this quarter that hindered your performance.

MY NOTES